ASAP
U.S.
Government
& Politics

By the Staff of The Princeton Review

princetonreview.com

Penguin
Random
House

The Princeton Review
110 East 42nd Street, 7th Floor
New York, NY 10017
Email: editorialsupport@review.com

Published in the United States by Penguin
Random House LLC, New York, and in Canada
by Random House of Canada, a division of
Penguin Random House Ltd., Toronto.

ISBN: 978-1-5247-5766-3
eBook ISBN: 978-1-5247-5771-7
ISSN: 2574-1195

Editor: Aaron Riccio
Production Editors: Kathy Carter and Melissa
Duclos
Production Artists: Deborah A. Silvestrini and
Craig Patches

Printed in the United States of America.

10 9 8 7 6 5 4 3 2 1

Editorial

Rob Franek, Editor-in-Chief
Casey Cornelius, VP Content Development
Mary Beth Garrick, Director of Production
Selena Coppock, Managing Editor
Meave Shelton, Senior Editor
Colleen Day, Editor
Sarah Litt, Editor
Aaron Riccio, Editor
Orion McBean, Associate Editor

Penguin Random House Publishing Team

Tom Russell, VP, Publisher
Alison Stoltzfus, Publishing Director
Jake Eldred, Associate Managing Editor
Ellen Reed, Production Manager
Suzanne Lee, Designer

Acknowledgments

Many thanks to the all-star developers who poured their time, expertise, and focus into this project, from Gina Donegan and Jennifer McDevitt to Thomas Broderick and Corinne Dolci.

Special acknowledgment also to the above-and-beyond contributions of our production editors Kathy Carter and Melissa Duclos, and to our production artists, Deborah A. Silvestrini and Craig Patches, for finding ways to fully realize our designs.

Contents

Get More (Free) Content

1 Go to **PrincetonReview.com/cracking.**

2 Enter the following ISBN for your book: 9781524757663.

3 Answer a few simple questions to set up an exclusive Princeton Review account. (If you already have one, you can just log in.)

4 Click the "Student Tools" button, also found under "My Account" from the top toolbar. You're all set to access your bonus content!

Need to report a potential **content** issue?

Contact **EditorialSupport@review.com.**
Include:
- full title of the book
- ISBN number
- page number

Need to report a **technical** issue?

Contact **TPRStudentTech@review.com** and provide:
- your full name
- email address used to register the book
- full book title and ISBN
- computer OS (Mac/PC) and browser (Firefox, Safari, etc.)

Once you've registered, you can...

- Get valuable advice about the college application process, including tips for writing a great essay and where to apply for financial aid

- If you're still choosing between colleges, use our searchable rankings of *The Best 382 Colleges* to find out more information about your dream school

- Check to see if there have been any corrections or updates to this edition

- Get our take on any recent or pending updates to the AP U.S. Government & Politics Exam

Introduction

What Is This Book and When Should I Use It?

Welcome to *ASAP U.S. Government & Politics,* your quick-review study guide for the AP Exam written by the Staff of The Princeton Review. This is a brand-new series custom built for crammers, visual learners, and any student doing high-level AP concept review. As you read through this book, you will notice that there aren't any practice tests, end-of-chapter drills, or multiple-choice questions. There's also very little test-taking strategy presented in here. Both of those things (practice and strategy) can be found in The Princeton Review's other top-notch AP series—*Cracking.* So if you need a deep dive into AP U.S. Government & Politics, check out *Cracking the AP U.S. Government & Politics Exam* at your local bookstore.

ASAP U.S. Government & Politics is our fast track to understanding the material—like a fantastic set of class notes. We present the most important information that you MUST know (or should know or could know—more on that later) in visually friendly formats such as charts, graphs, and maps, and we even threw a few jokes in there to keep things interesting.

Use this book any time you want—it's never too late to do some studying (nor is it ever too early). The book is small, so you can take it anywhere and crack it open while you're waiting for soccer practice to start or for your friend to meet you for a study date or for the library to open.* *ASAP U.S. Government & Politics* is the perfect study guide for students who need high-level review in addition to their regular review and also for students who perhaps need to cram pre-Exam. Whatever you need it for, you'll find no judgment here!

 *Because you camp out in front of it like they are selling concert tickets in there, right? Only kidding.

Who Is This Book For?

This book is for YOU! No matter what kind of student you are, this book is the right one for you. How do you know what kind of student you are? Follow this handy chart to find out!

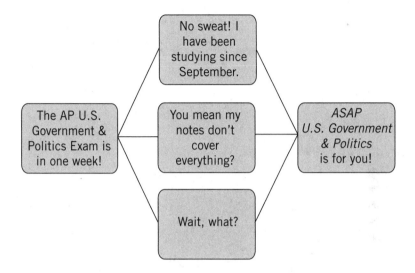

As you can see, this book is meant for every kind of student. Our quick lessons let you focus on the topics you must know, you should know, and you could know—that way, even if the test is tomorrow (!), you can get a little extra study time in, and learn only the material you need.

How Do I Use This Book?

This book is your study tool, so feel free to customize it in whatever way makes the most sense to you, given your available time to prepare. Here are some suggestions:

Target Practice

If you know what topics give you the most trouble, hone in on those chapters or sections.

ASK Away

Answer all of the Ask Yourself questions *first*. This will help you to identify any additional tough spots that may need special attention.

Three-Pass System

Start at the very beginning!* Read the book several times from cover to cover, focusing selectively on the MUST content for your first pass, the SHOULD content for your second pass, and finally, the COULD content.

---

 *It's a very good place to start.

Why Are There Icons?

Your standard AP course is designed to be equivalent to a college-level class, and as such, the amount of material that's covered may seem overwhelming. It's certainly admirable to want to learn everything—these are, after all, fascinating subjects. But every student's course load, to say nothing of his or her life, is different, and there isn't always time to memorize every last fact.

To that end, *ASAP U.S. Government & Politics* doesn't just distill the key information into bite-sized chunks and memorable tables and figures. This book also breaks down the material into three major types of content:

❗ This symbol calls out a section that has MUST KNOW information. This is the core content that is either the most likely to appear in some format on the test or is foundational knowledge that's needed to make sense of other highly tested topics.

💬 This symbol refers to SHOULD KNOW material. This is either content that has been tested in some form before (but not as frequently as MUST KNOW information) or that will help you to deepen your understanding of the surrounding topics. If you're pressed for time, you might just want to skim the SHOULD KNOW material, and read only those sections that you feel particularly unfamiliar with.

〰 This symbol indicates COULD KNOW material, but don't just write it off! This material is still within the AP's expansive curriculum, so if you're aiming for a perfect 5, you'll still want to know all of this. That said, this is the information that is least likely to be directly tested, so if the test is just around the corner, you should probably save this material for last.

As you work through the book, you'll also notice a few other types of icons.

❓ An Ask Yourself question is an opportunity to solidify your understanding of the material you've just read. It's also a great way to take these concepts outside of the book and make the sort of real-world connections that you'll need in order to answer the free-response questions on the AP Exam.

There's a reason why people say that "All work and no play" is a bad thing. These jokes help to shake your brain up a bit and keep it from just glazing over all of the content—they're a bit like mental speed bumps, there to keep you from going too fast for your own good.

Where Can I Find Other Resources?

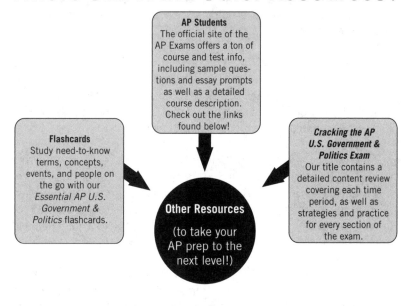

AP Students
The official site of the AP Exams offers a ton of course and test info, including sample questions and essay prompts as well as a detailed course description. Check out the links found below!

Flashcards
Study need-to-know terms, concepts, events, and people on the go with our *Essential AP U.S. Government & Politics* flashcards.

Cracking the AP U.S. Government & Politics Exam
Our title contains a detailed content review covering each time period, as well as strategies and practice for every section of the exam.

Other Resources

(to take your AP prep to the next level!)

Useful Links

- AP U.S. Government & Politics Homepage: https://apstudent.collegeboard.org/apcourse/ap-united-states-government-and-politics
- Your Student Tools: www.PrincetonReview.com/cracking
  See the "Get More (Free) Content" page for step-by-step instructions for registering your book and accessing more materials to boost your test prep.

CHAPTER 1

Constitutional Underpinnings

The United States is a global superpower, and yet many of its functions still rely upon a centuries-old document. In this chapter, we look at the various theories that were proposed for organizing the country, which ones made it into the Constitution, and how those articles have evolved throughout the years.

Influences on the Constitution !

The United States may have declared its independence in 1776, but it wasn't until 1789 that it actually ratified its Constitution. The ideas contained within that document did not materialize overnight, but were inspired by historical precedents in Europe and fierce debates. Although the framers of the Constitution rebelled to have freedom from England, they were still very much influenced by overseas ideas.

The European Enlightenment !

The European Enlightenment was an eighteenth-century philosophical movement that focused on the use of reason as opposed to a reliance on tradition when it came to solving social dilemmas. Below, you will find some of the ideas that helped the framers to challenge the conventional European wisdom regarding the relationship between a people and their government.

Natural Rights in the State of Nature !

The State of Nature describes a theoretical, pre-societal group of people who live without government. Philosophers like Thomas Hobbes and John Locke used this group to imagine what sort of natural rights an individual would have in this society and, consequently, why government might be necessary. Jean-Jacques Rousseau developed these ideas and defined the **social contract**—an abstract agreement between citizens in which they agree to forfeit certain freedoms in order to give authority to the government.

Thomas Hobbes

Humans have the right to fight for their own **life**, but such a chaotic, violent world would make that life "solitary, poor, nasty, brutish, and short." Therefore, some sort of government must exist to save us from the State of Nature!

John Locke

The State of Nature isn't so bad until conflicts arise over our other natural rights—**liberty** and **property**. As soon as we start to fight about freedom and possessions, we need government.

Jean-Jacques Rousseau

The government should have power only so long as it comes from the consent of the governed!

Social Contract Theory ❗

The Enlightenment ideals developed by Hobbes, Locke, and Rousseau formed the foundation of what is now called Social Contract Theory. Instead of studying the idealized way humans *should* behave (religion), it looked at how humans *actually* behave without governance: Are we selfish? Are we willing to share? Will we make sacrifices for others?

Enlightenment philosophers rejected the **divine right of kings**, which suggested that God chose who would rule, and instead argued that all humans were created with equal rights. They considered how individuals formed societies and, in particular, which freedoms they would give up in exchange for the benefits of being a part of a larger group. (For example, forfeiting the "freedom" to steal a peer's lunch money in exchange for the benefit of being able to attend school.)

 Ask Yourself...

Think about something you really want. What freedoms would *you* be willing to give up in order to get it?

Inspirations for the Constitution

Common Sense
Thomas Paine

described Enlightenment ideals in a way that the average British colonist living in America could understand. He penned the rallying cry "no taxation without representation" and urged colonists to break with with Britain and form a new nation.

1776

Declaration of Independence
Thomas Jefferson

described Enlightenment ideals in a way that King George could understand. Using language borrowed directly from Locke, Jefferson officially listed the colonists' complaints and filed for divorce from the British Empire.

1776

Charles de Montesquieu

saw the dangers of a single centralized government. He argued to divide political power into three branches—legislative, executive, and judicial.

1748

Voltaire

discussed freedom of religion as a natural right and revealed the dangers of having a government controlled by religious leaders. He argued for free speech and the separation of church and state.

1759

Jean-Jacques Rousseau

believed that the only justified government was one that was freely formed with the consent of the governed.

1762

 Rousseau's ideas and rallying cry are so embedded in American ideas that you might not even notice them, but you need look no further than *The Hunger Games* or *Divergent* to see the dangers of government without consent.

The Road to the Constitution

When the thirteen colonies that would become the United States declared their independence in 1776, they needed some sort of governing
documents—these were the Articles of Confederation, penned in 1777
and ratified in 1781. The failure of these articles to accommodate the
growth of the United States and its postwar needs would lead to the
writing of the Constitution in 1789.

The Articles of Confederation

The hasty laws established by the Articles of Confederation were sufficient during wartime, but as they had been designed to rid America of
any sort of centralized power, they were insufficient at handling the nation's growth. They provided for only a legislative branch of government,
so there was no way to enforce the laws or determine if laws were just.
Further, the government could not levy taxes, draft soldiers, or pay any
of the debts resulting from the Revolutionary War.

Shay's Rebellion

The case of Shay's Rebellion—in which a struggling farmer took up
arms against the government—demonstrates how and why the lack of
power in the Articles of Confederation was a problem for the United
States.

The weaknesses in the Articles of Confederation...	....caused...	...Shay's Rebellion.
The federal government could not levy taxes.	The federal government could not pay soldiers or debts left over from the Revolutionary War.	In 1787, Daniel Shay was struggling as a farmer in rural Massachusetts. He was a popular captain during the Revolutionary War but received no benefits as a veteran.
The federal government could not regulate or promote trade between the states.	Trade between the states went into decline. (This worsened when the British refused to trade with the new nation, their former vassal.)	Rural farmers suffered from high debt. Shay and his followers argued for flexibility, such as postponed payments or the permission to use crops as currency.
The federal government could not regulate laws passed by the states to ensure the rights of the people were protected.	State governments pass legislation to relieve the crisis. Some states pass pro-debtor laws, like the forgiving of debt or the printing of more paper money.	Massachusetts decided to take a hard line against debtors. Shay faces foreclosure and possible imprisonment for failure to repay debts.

The weaknesses in the Articles of Confederation...	....caused...	...Shay's Rebellion.
Both the federal and state governments can print money.	The constant printing of money (and rival currencies) causes its value to plummet.	The United States went into a state of economic crisis. Shay leads 1,200 people in an armed revolt against the government of Massachusetts.
The federal government cannot require states to contribute resources to a federal army.	The federal government is unable to intervene in the rebellion, leaving states with unchecked power to manage the crisis on their own.	The Massachusetts state militia sends 4,400 troops to end the rebellion. Four of Shay's militia are killed and over 1,000 are arrested.

Shay saw his rebellion as a continuation of the American Revolution: a struggle against unfair taxation from a remote governing power. To him, the revolution did not reflect a major change in the social order, but merely a shift in power from King George to the federal and state governments in the United States.

 Ask Yourself...

What were the differences in the ways that aristocrats and average citizens were treated between the American Revolution and the French Revolution?

 The next time you're sweating over writing an A+ paper, just remember that it took the brightest minds in America over a decade to turn their rough draft (Articles of Confederation) into a final draft (the Constitution).

Constitutional Convention of 1787 🛈

In order to address the issues of the Articles of Confederation, a group of elected delegates convened in Philadelphia, in 1787, to draft a new document forming a stronger central government. This document became the Constitution of the United States.

The framers of the Constitution were challenged by four key issues:

❶ Should each state have the same number of representatives in the legislative branch, or should representation be based on population?

❷ Which issues should be governed at the state level, and which issues at the federal level?

❸ How will the power of the presidency be limited to prevent tyranny?

❹ Should the government address slavery? If so, how?

Presiding:

George Washington
- Frustrated with the failings of the Articles of Confederation
- Worked in favor of a strong central government
- Unanimously elected as first president of the United States by attendees

Attending:

James Madison
- Argued consistently for the development of a powerful central government
- His Virginia Plan used as a partial blueprint for the Constitution
- His journals preserved the records of the Constitutional Convention

Alexander Hamilton
- Served as delegate to the Constitutional Convention from New York, but played a surprisingly small role in the debates themselves
- Wrote the Federalist Papers with James Madison to argue in favor of ratifying the Constitution
- Served as the first Secretary of the Treasury

Benjamin Franklin
- Helped draft the Declaration of Independence
- Negotiated an end to the war with Great Britain
- Antislavery, argued against giving voting rights only to white, male property owners (a practice known as "limited suffrage")

Declined:

Patrick Henry
- Proclaimed, "Give me liberty, or give me death!" during the revolution; feared power concentrating in a central government and industrial cities
- Did not attend the convention because he supported direct democracy and a rural, agrarian future for the country

John Adams
- Wrote the Massachusetts Constitution, laying the foundation for a two-house congress
- Did not attend the convention because he was serving as ambassador to Great Britain at the time

Samuel Adams
- Primary author of the Articles of Confederation
- Did not attend the convention because he objected to the creation of a strong central government

A Critique of the Constitution

In 1913, historian Charles Beard questioned the good intentions of the framers of the Constitution. Based on tax and census records, he suggested that these elite politicians designed a document to protect their own private wealth. George Washington, for example, lent the U.S. government money during the Revolutionary War and benefitted from the repayment of that war debt. Others criticize the Constitution on the basis of social contract theory—did slaves, for example, consent to give up their rights to the government? Rousseau wouldn't think so.

Separation of Powers: Legislative, Executive, and Judicial

As the framers were building the Constitution, they had two goals in mind: first, grant the federal government enough power to function; second, divide and limit the powers of government to prevent tyranny. To do this, they designed a government with power divided into three branches, each of which was designed to check and balance the powers of the other two branches.

NEWS

NEW CONSTITUTION DIVIDES POWER TO PREVENT TYRANNY

The framers of the Constitution challenged themselves with one of the most delicate balancing acts in social history—creating a federal government that was strong enough to hold the new nation of states together, but not so strong as to breed disconnected tyranny like the colonists experienced under British rule.

Inspired by Montesquieu, the framers began the Constitution by dividing the power of government into three branches:

• the legislative branch, responsible for writing laws
• the executive branch, responsible for heading the military and putting laws into action
• the judiciary branch, responsible for determining whether laws and executive actions are justified by the Constitution

The framers structured the branches of government with a system of checks and balances. Each branch of government works to limit the power of the other two, which ensures that none of them become overly powerful.

Checks and Balances ❗

JUDICIAL BRANCH (Supreme Court)

interprets the Constitution and other laws

Judicial Review
The Supreme Court supervises Congress and the president. Using the Constitution as a guide, the Supreme Court determines whether or not laws and executive actions are legal or unconstitutional, and therefore subject to reversal.

EXECUTIVE BRANCH (President)

administers the laws

may suggest laws

appoints ambassadors and other officials

conducts foreign policy

commands armed forces

Veto Power
The president has the power to veto any legislation written by Congress, meaning the president can prevent any newly written bill from becoming a law. (This power is limited. Congress can override a veto with enough votes.)

LEGISLATIVE BRANCH (Congress)

declares war

writes laws

ratifies treaties

grants money

confirms presidential appointments

Impeachment
Congress has the power to impeach the president or justices on the Supreme Court. Members can bring charges against federal judges or the president, hold a trial, and determine whether or not that individual should be removed from office.

There was so much fear about a large, centralized government that two political parties formed: the Federalists, who supported a strong central government, and the Anti-Federalists, who wanted to spread power among the states. The Federalists wrote a widely published series of papers arguing in favor of the Constitution. In *Federalist Paper #51,* James Madison argued that dividing power across three branches of government would prevent a strong centralized government from developing into tyranny.

The head of a parliamentary government (like that of Great Britain) is known as the prime minister, and he or she is a member of the legislative branch, selected from within the majority party to lead. The head of a federal government (like that of the United States) is the president, who is *not* a member of the legislature, and who does *not* vote to pass laws. Instead, the president either signs bills into law or vetoes them.

> **"**It may be a reflection on human nature, that such devices [checks and balances] should be necessary to control the abuses of government. But what is government itself, but the greatest of all reflections on human nature? If men were angels, no government would be necessary...you must first enable the government to control the governed; and in the next place oblige it to control itself."

> —James Madison, *Federalist Paper #51*

Expansion of Powers through Time ❗

The framers knew that they would not be able to predict the needs of future generations, and so the Constitution provides only a basic framework for the structure of the U.S. government. Some powers of government are explicit and known as **enumerated powers**, but others are vague, allowing the government to evolve over time. For example, "The power to declare war" has specific guidelines—it is enumerated. However, because Congress has the power to "make all laws which shall be necessary and proper," it is the Supreme Court's right to determine when a law is "necessary" and "proper." This flexibility allows each branch to exercise powers beyond those enumerated in the Constitution.

Congress and the Commerce Clause

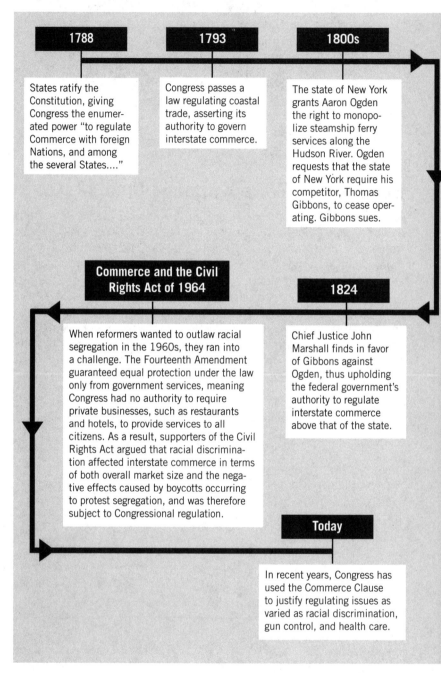

1788

States ratify the Constitution, giving Congress the enumerated power "to regulate Commerce with foreign Nations, and among the several States...."

1793

Congress passes a law regulating coastal trade, asserting its authority to govern interstate commerce.

1800s

The state of New York grants Aaron Ogden the right to monopolize steamship ferry services along the Hudson River. Ogden requests that the state of New York require his competitor, Thomas Gibbons, to cease operating. Gibbons sues.

Commerce and the Civil Rights Act of 1964

When reformers wanted to outlaw racial segregation in the 1960s, they ran into a challenge. The Fourteenth Amendment guaranteed equal protection under the law only from government services, meaning Congress had no authority to require private businesses, such as restaurants and hotels, to provide services to all citizens. As a result, supporters of the Civil Rights Act argued that racial discrimination affected interstate commerce in terms of both overall market size and the negative effects caused by boycotts occurring to protest segregation, and was therefore subject to Congressional regulation.

1824

Chief Justice John Marshall finds in favor of Gibbons against Ogden, thus upholding the federal government's authority to regulate interstate commerce above that of the state.

Today

In recent years, Congress has used the Commerce Clause to justify regulating issues as varied as racial discrimination, gun control, and health care.

The Supreme Court and Judicial Review

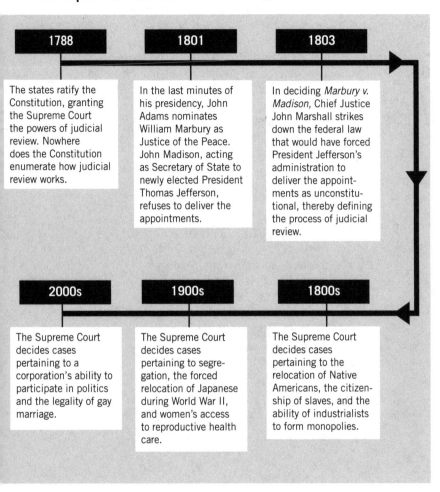

1788	1801	1803

1788: The states ratify the Constitution, granting the Supreme Court the powers of judicial review. Nowhere does the Constitution enumerate how judicial review works.

1801: In the last minutes of his presidency, John Adams nominates William Marbury as Justice of the Peace. John Madison, acting as Secretary of State to newly elected President Thomas Jefferson, refuses to deliver the appointments.

1803: In deciding *Marbury v. Madison,* Chief Justice John Marshall strikes down the federal law that would have forced President Jefferson's administration to deliver the appointments as unconstitutional, thereby defining the process of judicial review.

2000s	1900s	1800s

2000s: The Supreme Court decides cases pertaining to a corporation's ability to participate in politics and the legality of gay marriage.

1900s: The Supreme Court decides cases pertaining to segregation, the forced relocation of Japanese during World War II, and women's access to reproductive health care.

1800s: The Supreme Court decides cases pertaining to the relocation of Native Americans, the citizenship of slaves, and the ability of industrialists to form monopolies.

Common Law in a Constitutional Democracy

In the United States, the judicial branch has the unique responsibility to check the power of the people. To do so, they rely upon setting common law through **legal precedent**, previous legal decisions that pertain to the issue in question. For example, the functionality of the U.S. Supreme Court is defined by common law. The Constitution does not indicate how the Court should function; instead, Chief Justice John Marshall set the precedent when he decided *Marbury v. Madison* in 1803. Similarly, *Plessy v. Ferguson* set the common law standard of "separate but equal" to justify racial discrimination in 1896 before the Civil Rights Act of 1964 made segregation illegal.

Chief Justice John Marshall...is that name starting to sound familiar? Born in 1755 in Virginia, Marshall served in the Revolutionary War before beginning a career in law and being elected to Congress. In 1801, he became chief justice of the U.S. Supreme Court. During his 34-year tenure, he cemented his legacy in governmental philosophy by defining the process of judicial review.

The President and the Powers of War

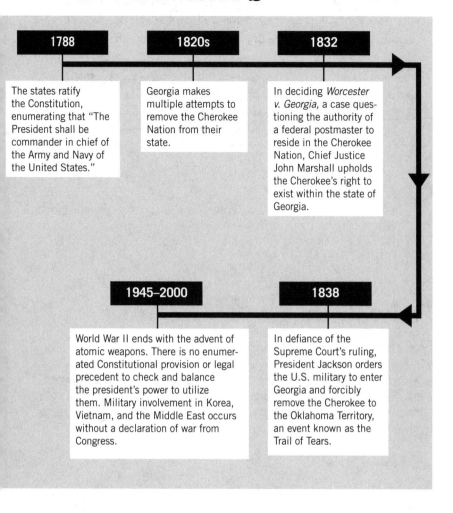

1788

The states ratify the Constitution, enumerating that "The President shall be commander in chief of the Army and Navy of the United States."

1820s

Georgia makes multiple attempts to remove the Cherokee Nation from their state.

1832

In deciding *Worcester v. Georgia,* a case questioning the authority of a federal postmaster to reside in the Cherokee Nation, Chief Justice John Marshall upholds the Cherokee's right to exist within the state of Georgia.

1945–2000

World War II ends with the advent of atomic weapons. There is no enumerated Constitutional provision or legal precedent to check and balance the president's power to utilize them. Military involvement in Korea, Vietnam, and the Middle East occurs without a declaration of war from Congress.

1838

In defiance of the Supreme Court's ruling, President Jackson orders the U.S. military to enter Georgia and forcibly remove the Cherokee to the Oklahoma Territory, an event known as the Trail of Tears.

"The decision of the Supreme Court has fell still born, and they find that it cannot coerce Georgia to yield to its mandate."

—President Andrew Jackson

Constitutional Underpinnings **19**

With the quote on the previous page, President Andrew Jackson was essentially daring Chief Justice John Marshall to enforce his decision as he decided to ignore the Supreme Court's decision and remove the Cherokee from Georgia. Some argue that this was an abuse of presidential power, and the Trail of Tears remains a tragic moment in the history of U.S. governance, but it does provide an excellent example of checks and balances at work. By invoking his enumerated power as commander in chief, President Jackson effectively checked the power of the Supreme Court.

Ask Yourself...

Look in a newspaper and identify some of the government's recent actions. Do you think those powers were enumerated in the Constitution? If not, what could the government have done differently?

Federalism

In addition to checks and balances, the framers of the U.S. Constitution relied on **federalism** to limit the government's power. Federalism is a concept that describes the division of governing powers between the federal government and state governments. In theory, this division is another safeguard against any single government power becoming tyrannical.

Federalism in the Constitution 🛈

Those powers that belong to the national government only are called delegated, expressed, or enumerated powers. Powers that belong exclusively to the states are called reserved powers. Those powers that are shared by the federal and state governments are called concurrent powers.

Federal Government—Enumerated Powers
- printing money
- regulating interstate and international trade
- making treaties and conducting foreign policy
- providing national defense
- managing Indian affairs
- declaring war
- providing postal service

Concurrent Powers
- collecting taxes
- building roads
- operating courts of law
- selling bonds to raise money for government programs
- establishing and maintaining courts

State Governments—Reserved Powers
- issuing licenses
- regulating of intrastate (within the states) businesses
- establishing local government
- regulating intrastate trade
- providing police services

A Closer Look at Federalism's Controversial Powers

In their efforts to keep the Constitution agreeable to all and flexible over time, the framers phrased some powers in broad terms. This has left certain portions of the Constitution open for often-controversial interpretation by the Supreme Court.

The Constitution

Article 1

Article VI

Tenth Amendment

Necessary and Proper Clause

The necessary and proper clause of the Constitution (Article I, Section 8) allows Congress to "make all laws" that appear "necessary and proper" to implement its delegated powers. This is also called the elastic clause. For example, there is nothing in the Constitution that creates the Federal Reserve System, which is the central bank for the United States. Neither is there any mention of a cabinet in the executive branch. Both the Federal Reserve System and the cabinet were created under the "necessary and proper" provision. The Federal District Courts and the Courts of Appeals were also created by congressional elaboration.

Supremacy Clause

Article VI defines the Constitution as "the Supreme Law in the Land" and requires conflicts between federal law and state law to be resolved in favor of federal law. State laws that violate the Constitution, federal laws, or international treaties can be invalidated through the supremacy clause.

Tenth Amendment

According to the Tenth Amendment, reserved powers include any that the Constitution neither specifically grants to the national government nor denies to the state governments. These powers are not listed in the Constitution; in fact, they are made up of all powers not mentioned in the Constitution.

Ask Yourself...

How does each of these three components of the Constitution tip the balance of power in favor of either the state or national government? Which components support each other, and which are contradictory?

Federalists vs. Anti-Federalists

Despite all of the compromises that were reached at the constitutional convention, acceptance of the Constitution was by no means assured. The states had to ratify it, as well. Supporters and opponents of the Constitution broke into two camps, Federalists and Anti-Federalists.

Federalists Alexander Hamilton, James Madison, and John Jay wrote a series of newspaper articles supporting the Constitution, collectively known as *The Federalist Papers*. These articles were designed to persuade the states of the wisdom of a strong central government coupled with autonomous political power retained by the states.

Anti-Federalists such as Thomas Jefferson opposed the creation of a stronger national government, arguing that a Constitution would threaten citizens' personal liberties and effectively make the president a tyrannical king.

In the Ring

Fighting for the Federalists

- President George Washington and Benjamin Franklin
- Framers Alexander Hamilton and James Madison
- Publishers who largely argued in favor of the Constitution, circulating newspapers and pamphlets between the states

Fighting for the Anti-Federalists

- Secretary of State Thomas Jefferson
- Patrick Henry, who said "Give me liberty, or give me death!" after the British passed the Stamp Act
- Farmers
- Those living in rural areas or on the frontier

Their Argument

- The Constitution is required to safeguard the independence colonists fought for during the Revolution.
- The nation needs a stronger federal government to
  ○ ensure domestic peace between states
  ○ promote welfare, commerce, and liberty within the states
  ○ provide for the common defense

Their Argument

- The Constitution centralizes too much power within the three branches of government and would lead to tyranny.
- The new federal government threatens to
  ○ impose new taxes and enforce them with the military
  ○ silence the citizens with inadequate representation
  ○ repress the rights of states and individuals

"The powers delegated by the proposed Constitution to the federal government are few and defined. Those which are to remain in the State governments are numerous and indefinite."

—James Madison, Federalist, Framer of the Constitution

The Constitution is "totally subversive of every principle which has hitherto governed us. This power is calculated to annihilate totally the state governments."

—George Mason, Anti-Federalist, Delegate from Pennsylvania

Federalist Paper #10

In *Federalist Paper #10,* James Madison argued that the size of the population would, in and of itself, provide protection from tyranny. He reasoned that because the federal government was responsible for a populous citizenry, that citizenry would inherently reflect a diverse pool of interests and priorities that would form factions. In a representative government, each faction would check and balance each other. For example, because farmers, merchants, factory owners, and bankers were all to be represented in government, they would regulate each other. None would allow a corrupt, tyrannical faction to take control of the government.

Constitutional Compromises 🔔

The Constitution was controversial when proposed and there were many debates, especially around the development of the legislative branch. Congress was intended to be the representative branch of government, ensuring that each citizen had a voice in government. But finding a fair way to select representatives proved difficult. Some states were more populous than others, so smaller states feared being overshadowed if representation was based on population. Northern states depended on industry and had densely populated urban centers, while southern states were rural, with agricultural economies that were dependent upon slave labor. Each group wanted to be sure that the new government would protect its interests.

As a result, the framers considered two strategies for selecting representatives:

The Virginia Plan

The large states seized the agenda at the beginning of the convention and proposed the Virginia Plan, a recipe for a strong government with each state represented proportionately to its population.

The New Jersey Plan

The small states worried that a government dominated by the large states wouldn't protect their interests, so they proposed the New Jersey Plan, under which each state would have an equal number of representatives.

The Connecticut Compromise

Eventually, the framers came up with what is known as the "Great Compromise" (or the "Connecticut Compromise"), which provides the framework for the U.S. Congress as it is currently structured: a bicameral (two-house) legislature. To appease the large-state supporters of the Virginia Plan, they created a House of Representatives, based on population. To satisfy the smaller states who had been backing the New Jersey plan, they also created a Senate, which featured two representatives from each state.

Three-Fifths Compromise

Another major conflict arose over the representation of slaves. Northerners felt that slaves, who could not vote, should not be counted when determining each state's number of representatives, while Southerners disagreed. The "solution" was the infamous Three-Fifths Compromise, in which the decision was made that slaves would count as three-fifths of a person when apportioning votes.

Debate and Ratification

Ratifying the Constitution was a dramatic, months-long process. Heated public debates questioned whether the federal government was usurping rights from state governments and acting in the best interest of the people. New York was the final state to ratify the Constitution after Alexander Hamilton offered the critical compromise in favor of the Federalist cause: a series of ten amendments known as the Bill of Rights would be added to the Constitution to protect individual freedoms from tyranny.

Amending the Constitution ❗

One reason that the Constitution has lasted more than 200 years is that it is flexible. Many of its provisions require interpretation, allowing the document to become more conservative or progressive as the times warrant.

There are two ways to amend, or change, the Constitution. First, a proposed amendment must be introduced to both houses of Congress and approved by a two-thirds majority in each. The amendment is then passed on to each of the fifty state legislatures. Three-fourths of the state legislatures must ratify (approve) the amendment for it to become part of the Constitution.

The Constitution allows for a second means of amendment. Two-thirds of the state legislatures could petition Congress to call a constitutional convention. Because no constitutional convention has taken place since the writing of the current Constitution, nobody knows for certain how extensively conventioneers would be allowed to alter the Constitution. Could they rewrite it entirely, or would they be restricted to amendments mentioned specifically in their petitions for a convention? Fear that a constitutional convention might lead to drastic alterations has persuaded many state legislators to oppose any call for a convention.

Proposal Methods	Ratification Methods
• Proposed amendment wins $\frac{2}{3}$ majority in the House and Senate	• $\frac{3}{4}$ of all state legislatures approve of the amendment
• A constitutional convention is called by $\frac{2}{3}$ of state legislatures. Any amendment can now be proposed at the convention	• $\frac{3}{4}$ of special state-ratifying conventions approve the amendment

The Bill of Rights 🄳

The ability to amend the Constitution was critical to it being ratified by all the states. Because there was so much fear that the strong federal government advocated by the Federalists would become tyrannical, the Anti-Federalists insisted on a series of amendments to explicitly limit the power of the government and protect the rights of the citizens. These rights included protecting individual freedoms, protecting the rights of the accused, and limiting the power of the federal government. In 1791, Virginia became the final state to ratify the first ten amendments, known as the Bill of Rights, and the U.S. Constitution was formed.

Main Ideas in the Bill of Rights 🄳

The Bill of Rights clarifies people's rights, puts restraints on government power, and defines what powers are held by the states.

	Amendment	Main Idea	Example
Protecting Individual Freedoms	1st	• Freedom of Speech/Press • Freedom of Religion • Freedom of Assembly & Petition	• Way too many to list here, but you can flip to page 203 for more!
	2nd	• Right to bear arms.	• *District of Columbia v. Heller* (2008) strikes down the handgun ban in Washington, D.C., and other federal enclaves.
	3rd	• The government cannot quarter soldiers in people's homes during peacetime.	• *Engblom v. Carey* (1982) finds in favor of striking prison guards whose homes had been illegally occupied by the National Guard.

	Amendment	Main Idea	Example
Protecting the Rights of the Accused	4th	• Law enforcement requires a warrant or probable cause for search and seizure. • The exclusionary rule prohibits illegally attained evidence.	• The Patriot Act (2001), passed by Congress after 9/11, arguably violates portions of the Fourth Amendment. • *United States v. Leon* (1984) establishes the **good faith exception**, whereby a judge can admit illegally obtained evidence if the officer is determined to have been acting in "good faith."
	5th	• People do not have to testify against themselves. • A grand jury must indict a defendant when a capital crime has occurred. • A person cannot be charged with the same crime more than once. (Double Jeopardy) • Government must fairly compensate people if it takes their property for public use. (Eminent Domain)	• *Miranda v. Arizona* (1966) rules that officers must inform suspects of their Fifth Amendment rights at the time of the arrest.

Constitutional Underpinnings

	Amendment	Main Idea	Example
Protecting the Rights of the Accused	6th	• Right to a speedy trial. • Right to a lawyer in federal cases.	• *Powell vs. Alabama* (1932) determines that defendants in federal cases have the right to council. Much later, the Supreme Court extends this right to *all* court cases.
	7th	• Right to trial by a jury of one's peers.	• *Ballew v. Georgia* (1978) decides that in a jury trial, a jury must have at least six members.
	8th	• Forbids cruel and unusual punishment.	• *Furman v. Georgia* (1972) temporarily finds that the death penalty violates the Eighth Amendment, but this decision is reversed four years later.
Limiting the Powers of the Federal Government	9th	• Even if a right is not listed in the Bill of Rights, it is still retained by the people.	• *Roth v. United States* (1957) rules that publishing obscenity was not one of the "rights retained by the people."
	10th	• All powers not given to the federal government by the Constitution remain with the states.	• *Gonzales v. Raich* (2005) allows the federal government to ban the use of medical cannabis that crosses state lines, as this would be in violation of the Constitution's Commerce Clause.

 The Bill of Rights is pretty straightforward, which is why we've used icons to keep things simple. But unless you're trying to make it easier for AP graders to skip through your Free Response Questions (giving you 0 points), make sure you write in full sentences, not emoji.

Hamilton's Bank Plan

After ratifying the Constitution, the new government still had to remedy the economic crisis of the 1780s that prompted Shay's Rebellion. President George Washington selected Alexander Hamilton, a successful financier during the Colonial Era, to be the first Secretary of the Treasury. Hamilton's plan, unveiled in 1791, utilized a variety of strategies to support the manufacturing and banking industries and to build trust in the economic security of the new nation.

The Pillars of Hamilton's Bank Plan

- Charter a national bank of the United States.
- Sell securities to investors to raise funds to pay states' war debts; repay investors with interest over time.
- Maintain a stable paper currency.
- Enact protectionist policies to support U.S. manufacturers through subsidies and tariffs.

Constructionism and the Bank Plan

Debate over Hamilton's plan revolved around a principle called **constructionism**. **Strict constructionists** believed that the federal government had rights only to the enumerated powers in the Constitution, whereas **loose constructionists** argued that under the necessary and proper clause, the federal government had the right to define new powers. Like the debate over federalism, this controversy divided the early government into two factions, those who believed Congress had the right to establish a national bank, and those who believed Congress did not have that right.

Strict Constructionists

Position: The Tenth Amendment states that any power not specifically delegated to the federal government is reserved for the states. As the Constitution nowhere authorizes a bank, the federal government has no right to charter a national bank.

Team Captain: Secretary of State Thomas Jefferson

Team Profile: Anti-Federalists, farmers, those living in Southern states (who had already repaid their war debts without assistance from the federal government).

Vision for the United States: A rural nation of farmers and artisans, where all citizens can participate in small, local government.

Loose Constructionists

Position: The Constitution gives Congress the power to make any laws "necessary and proper" to ensure the government and society can function. It is necessary and proper to charter a bank to provide economic stability.

Team Captain: Secretary of the Treasury Alexander Hamilton

Team Profile: Federalists, manufacturers, industrialists, and bankers living in northern states.

Vision for the United States: An industrialized nation with strong banks, manufacturing, and public credit maintained by a large federal government.

Perhaps you've heard of the hit Broadway musical *Hamilton?* It features an epic rap battle between Jefferson and Hamilton debating the merits of the bank plan.

Secretary of State Thomas Jefferson was the most vocal of those who accused bank supporters of being "a corrupt squadron of paper dealers." His concern stemmed from the fact that many of the members of Congress who voted in favor of the First National Bank stood to gain from it, as they had investments in public securities.

James Madison, despite co-authoring *The Federalist Papers* with Hamilton, argued that the plan to repay states' debts gave too much money and power to wealthy financiers like Hamilton himself. During his tenure as president, Madison checked the power of the legislative branch by temporarily revoking the bank's charter.

Despite the drama surrounding the First National Bank, Congress chartered the Second National Bank of the United States in 1816 in an attempt to control unregulated currency issued by state banks. In 1818, Maryland tried to tax the national bank, as it was conducting business within state borders. When James W. McCulloch, a federal bank agent working out of Baltimore, refused to pay, Maryland sued. Unanimously, the Supreme Court decided that the government *does* have the authority to charter a national bank, and that Maryland *does not* have the authority to tax the federal government. In his decision, Chief Justice John Marshall used both the Necessary and Proper Clause and the Supremacy Clause to justify his reasoning. This decision was critical to U.S. history in that it set the precedent for an elastic reading of the Constitution and further expansion of federal power.

Federalism After *McCulloch v. Maryland*

The boundaries of federal power have been contested through every era of U.S. history. Here is a timeline of major events that affected the authority of federal government:

1832	Tensions between Northern and Southern states deepen when South Carolina nullifies a federal tariff on British textiles. President Jackson requests legislation to mobilize federal troops to enforce the tariff, but Congress revises the tariff before confrontation occurs.
1861–1865	The Civil War reflects a major weakness in federal power. Seceded states in the South form the Confederate States in order to fight any authority from the federal government.
Late 1800s	The Industrial Revolution requires rapid infrastructure development in the form of roads, bridges, and canals. States accept more federal grants, oversight, and regulation.
1933	Under President Franklin Delano Roosevelt, Congress passes the New Deal, a suite of legislation designed to jump-start the economy during the Great Depression. Programs greatly expand federal oversight into state affairs and include infrastructure development, new agricultural policy, and funding for civic arts.
1964	Under President Johnson, Congress passes the Civil Rights Act, ending racial segregation in public spaces. Governments of southern states resist, arguing that the issue falls under the authority of state governments.
1995	Congress reenacts the Gun-Free School Zone Act of 1991. After being struck down by the Supreme Court as unjustified under the Interstate Commerce Clause, Congress includes new evidence as to the effects of the law on gun sales and the importance of education to interstate commerce.
1996	Under President Clinton, Congress passes Welfare Reform, decreasing federal oversight into how states allocate resources to those living below the poverty line.

Constitutional Underpinnings

Nullification is a constitutional principle first defined by Thomas Jefferson. In accordance with the philosophical ideal that the authority to govern comes directly from the people themselves, the Doctrine of Nullification says that the people, acting through state governments, also have the authority to take that power away. Government leaders from the South during the first half of the 1800s, like Vice President John C. Calhoun, thought nullification could be an effective means for Southern states to prevent the federal government from regulating their slave-based economy.

 Ask Yourself...

James Madison argued that states were "duty bound to resist" laws that they found unconstitutional. Do you agree? Can you think of any modern examples of states resisting legislation put forward by the federal government?

Federalism Today

So how do the state and federal governments actually work together to get the job done? Most legislation that comes out of Congress utilizes formal instructions that require the states to address certain issues, such as aiding the poor, cleaning the environment, improving education, and protecting the handicapped. These instructions are known as "mandates to the states." The federal government pays for these programs through grants-in-aid, which are outright gifts of money to the states. There are two kinds of grants, categorical and block.

	Categorical Grants	Block Grants
Provides:	Aid with detailed provisions from the federal government as to how it is to be spent.	Aid for broadly defined programs.
Examples:	Head Start, Medicaid, Food Stamp Program	Welfare, Community Development, Social Services
Supporters Say:	These grants allow the federal government to ensure that funds are going toward their intended use.	Decisions about how grant money should be spent should be left to the states because they are more aware than the federal government of the needs of their citizens.
Supported By:	Democrats, who traditionally favor strict regulation and oversight for the states.	Republicans, who traditionally favor the states' authority to administer federal law as needed in their states.

Dual Federalism vs. Cooperative Federalism

Early in U.S. history, the nation operated under a system known as **dual federalism**. Under dual federalism, the state and federal governments operated with equal authority but in different spheres. The states had authority to manage affairs within their borders, such as education and social services, while the federal government had authority to manage intrastate and international affairs, such as the construction of railways and the distribution of public land in the West. Think of dual federalism as a layer cake, with chocolate and vanilla flavors remaining distinct but working on different levels to create a unified cake.

Today, the United States operates under **cooperative federalism**. Under cooperative federalism, the state and federal governments work together to provide services to the citizens. For example, the federal government might set minimum education or health care standards and leave it up to the state governments to administer programs to the citizens through grants. In other words, under cooperative federalism, federal and state governments cooperate to solve social issues together, as opposed to delegating them to a single level of government. Think of cooperative federalism as a marble cake, in which chocolate and vanilla swirl and work together in each layer to create a unified cake.

Advantages of Federalism

- Mass participation: Constituents of all ages, backgrounds, races, and religions can participate by voting on both local and national issues.
- Regional autonomy: States retain some rights and have choices about public policy issues such as gun control, property rights, abortion, and euthanasia.
- Government at many levels: Politicians are in touch with the concerns of their constituents.
- Innovative methods: States can be laboratories for government experimentation, to see if policies are feasible.

Disadvantages of Federalism

- Lack of consistency: Differing policies on issues like gun control, capital punishment, and local taxes can clog the court system and create inequality in states.
- Inefficiency: Federalism can lead to duplication of government and inefficient, overlapping, or contradictory policies in different parts of the country.
- Bureaucracy: Power can be spread out among so many groups; it can result in corruption and a stalemate.

Democracy

Democracy is a form of government in which the power to make laws is exercised by representatives. For the framers of the Constitution, this concept was a central part of the blueprint for limited government: a system in which individuals—whether they're the president, a senator, or a justice—have little power without first earning the approval of the other branches of government or the people. In practice, the United States has utilized a blend of democratic styles.

Forms of Democracy

Representative Democracy: Trustee Model

Representative democracy, also known as **indirect democracy,** is the primary model of our current government. In this system, citizens select a delegate to represent them in the governing process. The United States uses the **trustee model**, in which citizens vote to select a representative based on his or her platform (a mixture of philosophies, ideologies, and policies) and merits as a leader. All of the elected representatives are then trusted to look out for the interests of those who voted for them (their constituents).

- BENEFIT: Individuals can elect knowledgeable and competent leaders to represent them in government and pass laws more efficiently than they would be able to in a direct democracy.
- CRITIQUE: Trustees inevitably have to invest working time and resources on getting elected, as opposed to addressing societal issues.
- EXAMPLES: John Adams first coined the term "representative democracy" in 1794 as he worked to form the federal government. Both the state and federal governments in the United States are representative democracies with senators and congressional representatives acting as trustees.

Representative Democracy: Delegate Model

Under the less common **delegate model**, the delegate's individual perspective is irrelevant and he or she works to literally communicate the will of the constituents. A delegate might poll these constituents to more accurately represent them during the legislative process.

- BENEFIT: The will of the people is concretely represented in government, without potential bias or corruption on behalf of the trustee.
- CRITIQUE: The people may lack the knowledge or empathy to make laws that benefit society as a whole, resulting in "mob rule" that could lead to tyranny or chaos.
- EXAMPLES: In the Electoral College system that is used to elect the president, each state is assigned a number of votes based on its population. After a state votes for president, the majority winner in that state wins *all* of the state's electoral votes, and a delegate casts those votes within the Electoral College according to the will of the voters.

Exception to the Rule
  o Maine and Nebraska reserve some Electoral College votes for the candidate who wins specific congressional districts as opposed to the popular vote in the state as a whole. There are a handful of Electoral College delegates that have chosen to vote *against* the popular vote in their states, but this is very rare and has never affected the outcome of an election.

Direct Democracy

Direct democracy is a system in which the citizens vote directly on any government law or action.

- BENEFIT: Individuals are more connected to and thereby more active with politics.
- CRITIQUE: This model is cumbersome, expensive, and difficult to monitor.
- EXAMPLES: Direct democracy was the first form of democracy used in New England town hall meetings during the Colonial Era. In modern America, some states (like California) allow individuals to put propositions (proposed laws) onto ballots that their peers—fellow citizens—can then vote for or against. This is often used for potentially controversial issues, such as gay marriage and cannabis legislation.

Theories About Democracy

Though currently held as the gold standard of government styles, democracy isn't so popular with everyone. Plato considered democracy to be a corrupt form of government. In his view, the common citizen is ignorant, self-interested, and unprepared for the responsibilities of government. For Plato, democracy could only end in tyranny or anarchy. Here are two common arguments.

FOR: Pluralist Theory

The Pluralist Theory of Democracy builds upon the ideas Madison put forward in *Federalist Paper #10,* holding that a large population will inevitably form factions, or interest groups, which will limit the influence of other factions and the government at large. Groups such as the National Education Association (NEA), the American Civil Liberties Union (ACLU), and the American Association of Retired Persons (AARP) all work to monitor the actions of the government to ensure the needs of their constituents are taken into account. Labor unions work in a similar way, protecting the interests of workers (teachers, nurses, or firefighters, for example) in negotiations with profit-minded employers.

AGAINST: Elite Theory

The Elite Theory of Democracy posits that even in a democracy, political power will centralize in the hands of the elite. In the United States, some consider wealthy factions to be "elites." For example, consider the efforts of the oil industry to block environmental regulations. Similarly, in his farewell address, President Eisenhower expressed concern over the military-industrial complex, suggesting that businesses selling goods to the U.S. army would drive the nation into international conflict for private profits.

CHAPTER 2

Political Beliefs

Everything Americans experience helps to inform their political beliefs. In this chapter, we'll look at the major beliefs and contributing factors to those beliefs, from personal circumstances (region, religion, school, race, income) to tumultuous social and economic shifts created by governmental policies, everyday interactions (with coworkers, friends, and family), and the way in which the news itself is presented.

Public Opinion !

By definition, a democratic government holds public opinion paramount in the decision-making process. As such, shifts in public opinion have caused radical changes in government policy in U.S. history, while public polling and voting practices continue to shape the state of the union.

Government Values from the Public Perspective !

The one thing that's been consistent about U.S. politics is how inconsistent it can be. From the earliest drafts of the Constitution up through the most recent elections, America has been defined by its changing views and policies. There are, however, five values that have largely held steady over the years, and which make up the heart of the philosophy behind U.S. government.

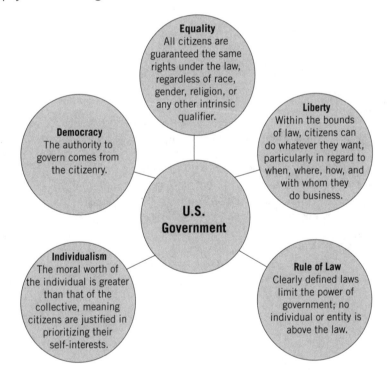

Equality
All citizens are guaranteed the same rights under the law, regardless of race, gender, religion, or any other intrinsic qualifier.

Democracy
The authority to govern comes from the citizenry.

Liberty
Within the bounds of law, citizens can do whatever they want, particularly in regard to when, where, how, and with whom they do business.

U.S. Government

Individualism
The moral worth of the individual is greater than that of the collective, meaning citizens are justified in prioritizing their self-interests.

Rule of Law
Clearly defined laws limit the power of government; no individual or entity is above the law.

An Outsider's Take on Democracy ❗

French diplomat and political scientist Alexis de Tocqueville's 1835 book *Democracy in America* ultimately rules in favor of democracy, but describes numerous concerns with the system.

- The concept of "equality" led citizens to expect total economic parity with their peers. This expectation led to rampant materialism and pervasive dissatisfaction associated with envy and shame.
- The **tyranny of the majority** occurs when people assume themselves to be right because they have the culturally dominant numbers on their side and not because they are ethically, morally, or sometimes even factually, correct.

"**D**emocracy encourages in the human heart a depraved taste for equality, which always impels the weak to want to bring the strong down to their level, and which reduces men to preferring equality in servitude to inequality in freedom."

—Alexis de Tocqueville

Evolving Political Opinions: The Industrial Revolution ❗

Scholars trace many contemporary social and political issues back to the Industrial Revolution, the era in which our modern economy took shape.

The Industrial Revolution

The advent of mechanized production, which spread from Europe at the end of the eighteenth century, caused a major shift in the United States, transforming it from a rural and agrarian society to an urban and industrialized one.

 Industrial Revolution

 Influx of New Inventions

- Spinning Jenny
- Cotton Gin
- Steam Engine
- Sewing Machine
- Telegraph

 Increased Productivity

 Increase in factory jobs, especially within the textile industry.

 Population Shift

 Growth of Cities

Government Response to the Industrial Revolution 😵

Though there were benefits to industrialization, such as an increasingly large and upwardly mobile middle class, the negative impacts to city life became readily apparent. Urban workers lived in squalor and were powerless against dangerous factory conditions and low pay.

To remedy this negative impact, a social and political movement known as **progressivism** advocated for the rights of workers and a more developed social safety net for all. Responding to the concerns of the citizens, the government took a variety of steps to reduce the consequences of industrialization.

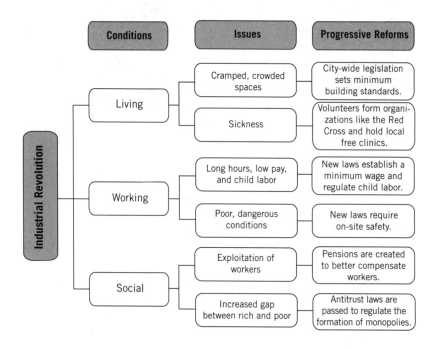

Capitalism in Question 💬

As the Industrial Revolution raged on, various industrialists and businessmen came to power and amassed a great deal of wealth. Some saw the negative effects of industrialization as the inherent flaws of free enterprise, a capitalist system in which the government does the minimum to regulate the economy. Others argued that the newly rich were in a unique position to reinvest in their community. Whether these titans of industry were viewed as heroes or villains often depended on how they gained and spent their money.

Robber Barons—Villains vs.	Captains of Industry—Heroes
• Drain natural resources	• Establish factories and increase productivity
• Pay poor wages and force poor working conditions	• Create jobs and raise standard of living
• Drive competitors to ruin	• Expand the market
• Steal from public to gain personal wealth	• Donate to philanthropic causes

Evolving Political Opinions: Roaring Twenties and Great Depression ❗

The 1920s proved a volatile decade for politics and public opinion. When World War I ended in 1918, many Americans were disillusioned with foreign affairs and took an isolationist attitude toward economics and public policy. At the same time, industrialization brought increased developments in communication technology, so more citizens were better informed about politics than ever. As a result, the government faced increased scrutiny as the nation experienced the worst economic crisis of U.S. history.

Public Opinion during the 1920s

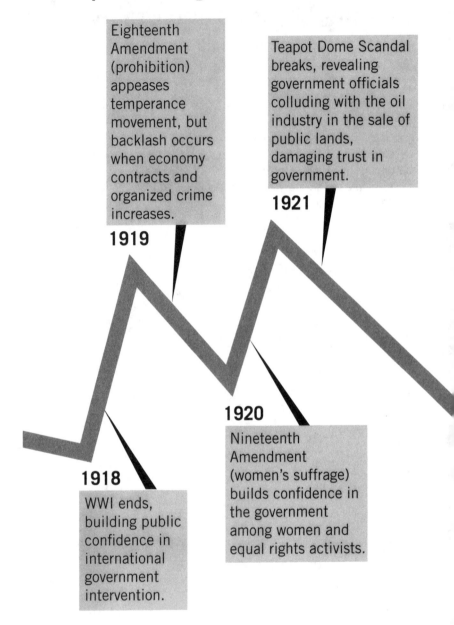

Eighteenth Amendment (prohibition) appeases temperance movement, but backlash occurs when economy contracts and organized crime increases.

1919

Teapot Dome Scandal breaks, revealing government officials colluding with the oil industry in the sale of public lands, damaging trust in government.

1921

1920

Nineteenth Amendment (women's suffrage) builds confidence in the government among women and equal rights activists.

1918

WWI ends, building public confidence in international government intervention.

Scopes Trial affirms a state law forbidding evolution to be taught in schools; this decision decreases confidence among those committed to evidence-based government policy.

1925

Stock market crashes, causing a crisis in confidence in free enterprise government policy.

1929

1928

Kellogg-Briand Pact affirmed by all major world powers, thus building confidence in international government intervention.

1924

Stock prices increase, raising confidence in free enterprise government policy.

Political Beliefs

How Industrialization Changed the United States

The Industrial Revolution made the United States an economic power-house, but it also forced the government to take a more active role in the lives of citizens. For the first time, social welfare was a priority of the federal government.

The Great Depression ❗

On October 29, 1929, or "Black Tuesday," the stock market crashed. This event marked the beginning of the Great Depression. Many faulted the government for the Great Depression, arguing that politicians didn't do enough to regulate an inflated banking system. As a result, the start of the Great Depression marked a major shift in popular opinion away from free enterprise policies and toward a federal government that more closely regulated the economy.

Effects of the Great Depression 💬

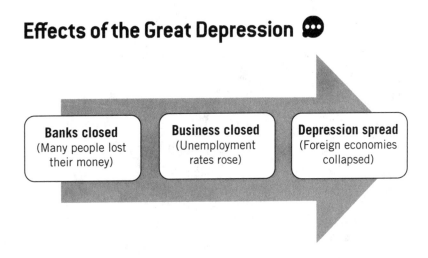

Banks closed
(Many people lost their money)

Business closed
(Unemployment rates rose)

Depression spread
(Foreign economies collapsed)

The Great Depression was a time of severe economic downturn. Consumers lost confidence in the market, so spending and investing declined sharply. The rippling effects of the crisis led to many cases of homelessness, sickness, and even starvation. The tariffs meant to stabilize the country's trade only resulted in spreading the damage abroad, grinding the global economy to a halt.

Realignment 💀

Many Americans blamed Republican President Herbert Hoover for the disaster, and they responded by electing overwhelming numbers of Democrats to every level and branch of government, such that Republicans became the minority party and Democrats became the majority. This shift, which saw Franklin Delano Roosevelt (FDR) inaugurated in 1933 and which caused individual coalitions to defect from one party to another, is known as **realignment.**

New Deal policies helped establish an era of Democratic governance. For example, between 1928 and 1932, Democrats went from holding 38% to 72% of seats in the House of Representatives. Democratic presidential candidates went on to win seven of the next nine elections.

FDR 🔄

FDR offered hope and conciliation, and in his first inaugural speech, coined the memorable phrase "the only thing we have to fear is fear itself." The immediate actions he took to end the crisis would ultimately see him elected a record-breaking four times.

The New Deal 😶

Roosevelt's New Deal (1933–1938), which relied on federal power, was enacted shortly after he took oath as president. From March through June of 1933, or the "First Hundred Days," FDR passed 15 bills, forming the backbone of the New Deal. The plan included a number of policy reforms and programs that would help the United States eventually recover from the Depression. Social Security was among the most noteworthy measures of the New Deal. The plan also included work and emergency relief programs as well as banking reform laws, among others.

Some Major New Deal Initiatives	
Agricultural Adjustment Act (AAA)	Aided farmers by paying them to decrease production, increase prices for crops, and reduce crop surpluses
Civilian Conservation Corps (CCC)	Reduced unemployment by providing 250,000 young males with jobs, generally in national parks and forests
Federal Deposit Insurance Commission (FDIC)	Backed all bank deposits up to $2,500 so that consumers no longer had to worry that another bank failure would deplete their savings
Public Works Administration (PWA)	Funded construction of various public works projects throughout the United States, such as airports, hospitals, and schools
Tennessee Valley Authority (TVA)	Generated electric power, controlled floods in the Tennessee River Valley, and provided jobs

Although some controversy surrounded FDR's initiative, the New Deal proved successful in many ways, providing thousands of Americans with short- and long-term relief and restoring the public's faith in the efficacy of government intervention in the economy.

Evolving Political Opinions: The Cold War and Beyond ❗

World War II marked a high point in the public's attitude toward the government as the citizenry was propelled out of the Great Depression and united in the struggle against Germany, Italy, and Japan. However, later during the Cold War, the looming threat of nuclear annihilation and communist expansion led many Americans to live in fear. This had a deep impact on their opinions about governmental policy, as well as their trust of the United States itself. Two events that occurred during the Cold War, the Vietnam War and the Watergate Scandal, had particularly negative consequences on the trust U.S. citizens have in their government.

The Vietnam War 💬

The Vietnam War, fought between the communist government of North Vietnam and the capitalist government of South Vietnam, lasted from 1954 through 1975. As part of its containment policy, the United States eventually (and officially) entered the war in 1964, fighting on the side of the anti-communist South.

In response to a set of confrontations that occurred between North Vietnam and the United States, Congress passed the **Gulf of Tonkin Resolution** in August of 1964. It gave the president the broad powers to commit unlimited numbers of troops for an unlimited length of time in the Vietnam conflict without a declaration of war from Congress. As casualties among U.S. soldiers increased in the late 1960s, President Johnson was unable to bring the war to a conclusion. Strong criticism of his handling of the war led to a general lack of support for his policies, undermining his ability to govern. Many Americans eventually protested U.S. involvement in the war, questioning the motives that brought the nation into armed conflict.

After years of fighting and over 58,000 American deaths, the United States withdrew from Vietnam in 1975 as North Vietnamese troops took control of South Vietnam.

The Vietnam War was the first "television war." During prior conflicts, such as the Korean War, TVs existed, but technology and the scope of people reached by this form of media were limited. As news broadcasts depicted the horrors of war and terror in Vietnam, the anti-war movement ignited among Americans.

American court cases related to the Vietnam War:

Case (year)	Incident	Verdict
Tinker v. Des Moines (1969)	Iowa students were suspended for wearing black armbands in protest of Vietnam War.	The court ruled suspension unconstitutional, stating the public school students do not "shed their constitutional rights at the schoolhouse door."
New York Times v. U.S. (1971)	Defense Department employee Daniel Ellsburg leaked sensitive data indicating that the war was going poorly; the government tried to prevent the publication of the "Pentagon Papers."	The court ruled that executive efforts to prevent the publications violated the First Amendment.
Lloyd Corporation v. Tanner (1972)	Shopping mall owners wanted to throw out war protestors.	Malls were declared private, rather than public, spaces. Mall owners were allowed to throw out protestors, who have substantially fewer rights in private establishments.

The Watergate Scandal ●●●

NEWS

WATERGATE SCANDAL

File photo

Spies working for President Richard Nixon's 1972 reelection campaign are caught breaking into the Democratic National Headquarters at the Watergate Hotel. Other illegal activities undertaken by the Nixon White House are now synonymous with the name "Watergate."

IMPEACHMENT?

Yes No

57% of Americans believed the president should be removed from office, which led Nixon to resign the presidency in 1974. He was the first and only U.S. president to do so.

The Watergate Scandal further eroded the trust Americans placed in their government, especially as it came out that Nixon had been actively using executive privilege to cover up evidence, until finally being checked by the Supreme Court. In the post-Watergate years, during the subsequent Ford and Carter administrations, many citizens grew wary and weary of the executive branch.

Voting, Polling, and Public Opinion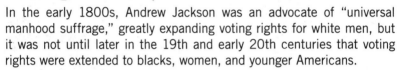

Another trend that has affected public attitudes toward government is the expansion of voting rights. Despite assertions that all men are created equal, the framers of the Constitution had a very narrow definition of citizens, especially among those who would have the right to vote. Though there were differing perspectives, in most states voting was restricted to land-owning, white males. Over time, repressed groups have fought and earned the right to vote, thus increasing participation and confidence in government.

Suffrage-Related Amendments

In the early 1800s, Andrew Jackson was an advocate of "universal manhood suffrage," greatly expanding voting rights for white men, but it was not until later in the 19th and early 20th centuries that voting rights were extended to blacks, women, and younger Americans.

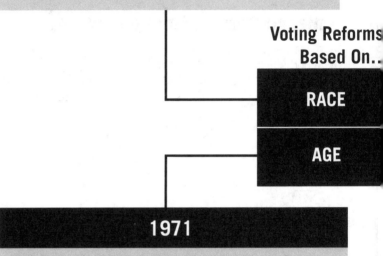

1870

After the Civil War ended in 1865, Congress abolished slavery (with the 13th Amendment), and guaranteed citizenship to all without regard to race, color, or previous condition of servitude with the 14th Amendment, but it was not until the passage of the **15th Amendment** that a black man's right to vote was federally protected. (This did not stop some states from working to make it difficult to do so, as with the 1883 passage of segregationist Jim Crow laws.)

Voting Reforms Based On..

RACE

AGE

1971

In response to the Vietnam War and a series of youth-led protests that called out the hypocrisy of being old enough for war but too young to vote, the **26th Amendment** lowered the voting age from 21 to 18. Due to the question of whether Congress or states had the right to set voter qualifications, it was necessary to pass this law directly as an amendment to the Constitution. (Fun fact: this amendment was ratified in just over two months, faster than any other.)

1920

A few states allowed women the right to vote—New Jersey, for instance, permitted this from 1776 to 1807, and Wyoming granted this right to all women in 1869. However, it wasn't until the **19th Amendment** was passed that all women in the United States could vote.

Voting Reforms Based On...

GENDER

INCOME/ INTELLIGENCE

1964

Certain states tried to deprive blacks of their voting rights by imposing literacy tests and poll taxes (fees that must be paid in order to vote). To allow poor, illiterate whites to vote, some states passed grandfather clauses that exempted from these restrictions anyone whose grandfather had voted. Grandfather clauses effectively excluded blacks whose grandparents had been slaves and therefore could not have voted. This practice was barred in 1964, with the passage of the **24th Amendment**, and the 1965 Voting Rights Act not only did away with literacy tests, but prohibited states from changing voting procedures without federal permission.

Civics 〰

Voting is the civic responsibility at the center of any functioning democracy. **Civic duties** (like jury duty and the payment of taxes) are the actual legal requirements for citizens, whereas **civic responsibilities** (like voting in elections or recycling) are largely unforced ideals that, if followed, would better help the country to flourish.

Factors That Influence Public Opinion ❗

The way in which people learn about politics as they grow and mature is known as **political socialization**. Thanks to the support of the First Amendment, which protects freedom of expression and promotes political tolerance, there are a wide variety of beliefs and ideologies that coexist in America.

Exposure to political ideologies begins in the home, but the views Americans adopt (or reject) may be reinforced or called into question by religious, academic, and workplace experiences. Underlying factors, such as geographical location and ethnicity, can also influence the development of one's personal politics. Here are just a few examples.

Home

Most people affiliate with the same political party as their parents.

Religion

Religious beliefs can impact individuals' lives. For instance, Jews tend to vote for liberal policies. Catholics do, too, except when social issues are involved. Then, they often have conservative positions.

School

Exposure to history and the varied perspectives of teachers and peers leads many to question their social and political assumptions for the first time, sometimes radically so.

Workplace

If a political party is seen to be working against the interests of an industry (Wall Street) or a powerful union (United Auto Workers), individuals may shift to the opposing party.

Race/Ethnicity

Blacks and Hispanics have been more likely to back liberal social programs, whereas Cuban Americans have tended to vote more conservatively.

Region

Not all states have the same needs, and the residents of a small rural state are likely to develop political views that are more socially conservative than those from large urban centers.

Income Level

Those with more money are often supportive of broad liberal goals like racial equality, but they are fiscally conservative. Poorer Americans often focus on immediate goals, such as financial reform and social welfare.

Gender

There isn't a specific split based on gender alone, but in combination with other factors like race and age, some trends show up, like the statistic that married women are more likely than single women to vote conservatively.

Place and Public Opinion

Historically, geography has been a strong predictor of public opinion. Prior to and during the Civil War, opinions could be mapped along sectionalist lines, with northern, southern, and frontier state boundaries marking changes in attitudes about slavery and the role of the federal government. During the 20th century, minority populations migrated from the South to urban industrial centers, causing the southern states to shift toward conservatism and urban, coastal regions to become increasingly liberal. Meanwhile, states such as Ohio and Pennsylvania, known for industrial manufacturing, formed the "rust belt," a concerted bloc of pro-union voters.

Today, political commentators have coined the term "urban archipelago" to describe the geographic relationship between liberalism and conservatism. Regardless of region or state, densely populated urban centers form "islands" of liberalism among "oceans" of conservative, rural areas.

Public Opinion in the Two-Party System

Although there is a broad spectrum of political beliefs in this country, many opinions—no matter how extreme—can often be expressed within the boundaries of the two most dominant political parties in the country, the Democrats (liberals) and Republicans (conservatives). Think of these organizations like the colors in a printer—you can get just about any color, but they come from a limited mixture of specific groups. This two-party system is known as **bipartisanship.**

Left-wing, liberal Democratic tendencies	Issue	Right-wing, conservative Republican tendencies
Favor legalized access	Abortion	Favor restricting access
Favor lenient sentencing & greater efforts at rehabilitation	Crime	Favor stricter enforcement & sentencing
Favor greater government subsidies or full socialization	Healthcare	Keep healthcare a private industry with only limited government involvement
Support gay marriage	Gay rights	Oppose gay marriage
Support gun control	Gun control (2nd Amendment)	Oppose gun control
Favor expansion	Immigration	Favor limitation and strict enforcement
Favor diplomacy, keep military budgets small during peacetime	Military spending	Fund military, favor strong military image
Believe broad regulation necessary to check corporate abuses	Regulation of business	Believe only limited regulation necessary
Favor separation of church & state	Religion	Oppose separation of church & state
Favor graduated income tax, fees, sales taxes for well-funded government programs	Taxation	Favor keeping taxes low & keeping budgets small
Favor more lenient laws & programs	War on Drugs	Favor stricter laws & programs
Favor expansion	Welfare	Favor limits and/or cuts

Polls Measure Public Opinion ❗

- Polls aim to determine public opinion by speaking to a smaller, **representative** sample, much as the 435 members of the House of Representatives aim to express the country's opinions. When performed correctly, a poll can approximate the opinions of 300 million Americans by polling a mere 1,500 of them.
- **Random sampling** is used to select that smaller group, and when polling by phone, the numbers are dialed at random to minimize bias. In-person **exit polls** work in the same fashion.
- Questions should be carefully worded and must remain both objective—no opinion is expressed by the question itself—and closed-ended. A specific question with a yes/no answer (for example, "Do you approve of the death penalty?") leaves little room for misinterpretation.
- Because polls are random and representative, they use a **margin of error** to express their results. A **sampling error** of ±4% suggests that if the poll reports that 60% of Americans are for something, that number may be anywhere from 56% to 64%.

Votes Enact Public Opinion ❗

While voting rights have been largely expanded over the last century, not all people who are eligible to vote actually do so. Since 1971, all U.S.-born, or naturalized, citizens aged 18 and over have had the right to vote. Americans are not required to vote by law, which is one of many factors contributing to low voter turnout rates in the United States.

Voting Statistics (as of 2012)

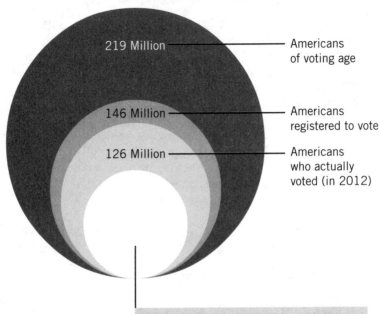

219 Million — Americans of voting age

146 Million — Americans registered to vote

126 Million — Americans who actually voted (in 2012)

Voter participation becomes even lower during midterm elections; in 2014, fewer than 40% of all eligible voters participated.

Demographic factors can influence voting patterns. For instance, the more educated a person is, the more likely he or she is to vote. Age also tends to significantly influence voting patterns: Americans over 40 are the most likely to vote while newly eligible voters (between the ages of 18 and 20) are the least likely to vote. Other demographic features affecting voting behaviors include ethnicity/race, gender, and religion. Voter turnout is also influenced in part by how close a race is: voters are less likely to vote when they believe they know who will win the election

Various legislation can also affect voter turnout. The National Voter Registration Act (1993), also known as the Motor Voter Act, made voting easier by allowing people to register to vote at the same time they apply for a driver's license. Conversely, the photo ID laws enacted in some areas at the state level depress voter turnout by requiring voters to show a photo ID before voting. These photo ID laws are controversial, with those supporting them saying such laws reduce voter fraud and those opposing them saying the measures decrease voting by impoverished Americans.

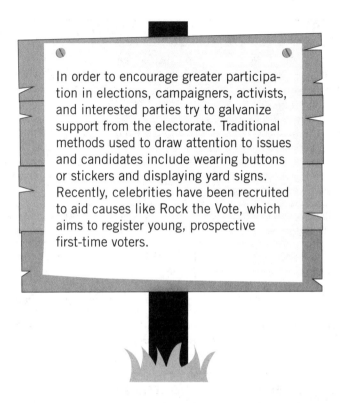

In order to encourage greater participation in elections, campaigners, activists, and interested parties try to galvanize support from the electorate. Traditional methods used to draw attention to issues and candidates include wearing buttons or stickers and displaying yard signs. Recently, celebrities have been recruited to aid causes like Rock the Vote, which aims to register young, prospective first-time voters.

Other Forms of Political Participation 🗯️

For many, political participation goes beyond voting. The following are further opportunities for citizens (and in some cases noncitizens) to take an active role in the governing process:

- Donate to a specific campaign, political action committee, or non-government interest group that promotes specific causes.
- Volunteer for a campaign or cause.
- Participate in local government, like the school board or city council.
- Run for local, state, or federal office.

As new forms of social media continue to create more accessible forums for public discourse, activism and outreach become more common.

SPLIT-TICKET VOTING

Split-ticket voting—voting for a presidential candidate of one party and legislators of the other—has grown more common. This practice leads to divided government, when one party controls the Senate or House or both and the other controls the White House. An example of this comes from the composition of the government as of 2015: following the 2014 elections, Republicans had House and Senate majorities, while Democrats controlled the White House. This situation can create policy gridlock because these two branches are often at odds with each other. Conversely, it can cause them to work together in the creation of moderate public policy. (You can only vote for senators and representatives from your area, so ballots will differ from state to state.)

PRESIDENT AND VICE PRESIDENT Vote for one team	U.S. SENATOR Vote for one	U.S. REPRESENTATIVE Vote for one
⬭ ELLIE PHANT AND NUMERO DOS Republican Party	⬭ REDD SABLE Republican Party	⬭ HELEN RUDDYMORE Republican Party
⬭ DON KEYSTONE AND CANDY DATE, THE SECOND Democratic Party	⬭ MARGARET LE BLEU Democratic Party	⬭ IRIS TUFTS Democratic Party
⬭ JADE S. KERMIT AND EMMY R. ALDER Green Party	⬭ VERA DANT Green Party	⬭ AVI C. ADO Green Party

ABSENTEE VOTING

If registered voters are unable to vote on election day, they may request an absentee ballot. Americans living abroad, military members, and persons with disabilities are some of the most common populations that use absentee voting. Absentee voting laws vary among states. If a voter does not have a valid reason for needing to vote in this fashion and does not want to go to the polls on election day, he or she may take advantage of other nontraditional voting methods such as early voting or vote-by-mail.

CHAPTER 3

Political Parties, Interest Groups, Mass Media

America is structured as a representative democracy, in which those who have been elected enact the political will of their constituents. However, because there are so few representative seats available, many of which are fiercely contested, others who want a seat at the table and some measure of control over the laws and policies that will affect them must find other means of influence. In this chapter, we'll look at some of the behind-the-scenes actors who work to ensure that those who are elected best represent their political party's policies or their interest group's freedoms. We'll also look at the mass media, which seeks to promote officials or hold them accountable on behalf of their readers.

Political Parties and Elections

Due to fiercely contested and prohibitively expensive campaigns, as well as the basic checks and balances of government, political parties are often formed. Political parties are a coalition of individuals who share a "platform" of ideas and pool their resources to ensure that the people who are elected best represent their policies and beliefs; these parties help to bridge the gap between regular citizens and elected officials.

Functions of Political Parties ❗

Function	Example(s)
Recruit/Nominate Candidates	• Finds like-minded candidates to run for local office. • Determines whom to support at the state/national level by holding a primary election.
Educate/Mobilize Voters	• Spreads information to support their candidate. • Creates attack ads to harm the reputation of the other party's candidate. • Pulls from decades of data to find the most vulnerable districts, those that can be "flipped" from one party to another.
Raise Money/Provide Campaign Funds	• Pools resources on behalf of a candidate to get around Federal Election Commission (FEC) caps on individual donations to a candidate. • Frees up candidates to do things *other* than fundraise.

ASAP U.S. Government & Politics

Organize Government Activity	• Splits the leadership and committees of House, Senate, and even state legislatures along party lines (what we call "partisanship") to present a unified message for their party. • Maintains voter blocs to help politicians reach necessary majorities on legislation. • Discourages individuals from voting outside party lines by threatening to withdraw future support.
Find Common Ground	• Appeals to a variety of smaller groups to consolidate power and exert more control. (The Republican Party, for example, aims to represent both religious social-conservatives and libertarians.)
Maintain Checks and Balances	• Holds the other party, especially the one with a majority, accountable for their votes by threatening to rehash those decisions during biennial reelection campaigns. (This approach is called being part of the loyal opposition.)

Political Parties, the "Necessary Evil" 💬

Some framers of the Constitution, like George Washington, were firmly against the notion of political parties, but others accepted the inevitable growth of "factions" in American politics:

> "Liberty is to faction, what air is to fire, an aliment without which it instantly expires. But it could not be a less folly to abolish liberty, which is essential to political life, because it nourishes faction, than it would be to wish the annihilation of air, which is essential to animal life, because it imparts to fire its destructive agency."
>
> —James Madison, *Federalist #10*

Party Structure ❗

When you come across an anthill, you know there's a lot going on underneath the surface. The same is true for political parties. In the Political Party Anthill, review the independent parts that make up America's major political parties.

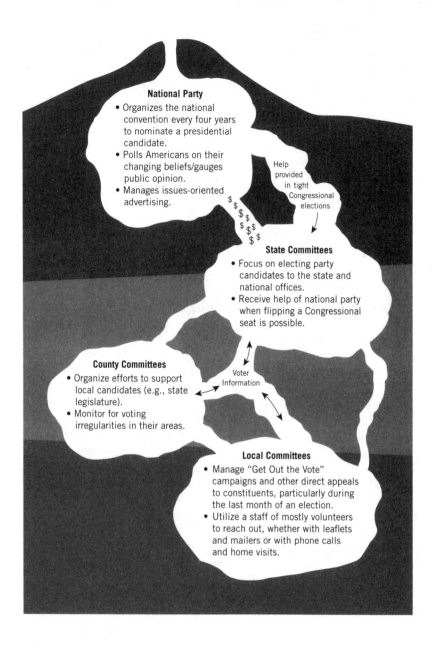

National Party
- Organizes the national convention every four years to nominate a presidential candidate.
- Polls Americans on their changing beliefs/gauges public opinion.
- Manages issues-oriented advertising.

Help provided in tight Congressional elections

$ $ $ $ $ $ $ $ $

State Committees
- Focus on electing party candidates to the state and national offices.
- Receive help of national party when flipping a Congressional seat is possible.

County Committees
- Organize efforts to support local candidates (e.g., state legislature).
- Monitor for voting irregularities in their areas.

Voter Information

Local Committees
- Manage "Get Out the Vote" campaigns and other direct appeals to constituents, particularly during the last month of an election.
- Utilize a staff of mostly volunteers to reach out, whether with leaflets and mailers or with phone calls and home visits.

 If you find ants, party hierarchy, or both to be disconcerting, take a five-minute break here and watch some soothing footage of an innocent animal of your choice. (We recommend the sloth.)

A Note on Hierarchy

Although the organizations of each level of the party system feed into one another, these are largely autonomous organizations, each of which serves a different function. State and local organizations often cooperate with the national level, but may sometimes prioritize their own interests.

For example, a state or local political party shares voter information with the national party when the national party steps in to help on a tight race. In these cases, the national party can use its "war chest" of donations to help target undecided voters.

The Two-Party System ❶

The American party system has been largely dominated by two major parties. That's because **almost** every election is decided by first-past-the-post voting. In these cases, the candidate who receives at least 50.1% of the vote wins. This rule makes it extremely difficult for smaller parties to win elections, whether in bigger races that leave them underexposed or in local races for which voting districts may have been defined to favor the current majority party.

The other electoral method commonly used is the two-round system. In contrast to first-past-the-post voting, the two-round system allows for a run-off election after initial voting occurs, although the details through which the run-off occurs vary. In France, any candidate receiving over 12.5% of the initial vote is on the ballot in the run-off; in the Ukraine, only the two highest vote winners in the initial election are allowed to participate. In the US, runoff elections are most commonly used to select officials at the city and state level, where there may be many lesser-known candidates competing for the same position. Nationally, ten states require that during the primary season a candidate can only win their party's nomination with at least 50%, so these states often hold primary runoffs during tightly contested years.

The Big Exception 🔵

In a presidential election, the winner is decided through the state-by-state votes of the Electoral College. The candidate who first gains 50.1% of these votes wins (as of 1964, that's 270 of 538), but due to close contests and disproportionate populations, that has resulted in several situations in which the winner of the popular vote did not end up becoming president.

The Two-Party System: Advantages

 As each party represents roughly half of the nation, it must create a coalition within its membership and with the other party.

 Each party acts as a check on the other.

 With fewer options, voters can more easily make an informed decision.

 A national government is generally more consistent when governed by a single political party and not a coalition.

The Two-Party System: Disadvantages

 Outside views are suppressed to create a unified party platform.

 Gridlock is more common.

 Voters may be unable to find a party that truly represents their beliefs.

 The expense of running a campaign and difficulty in reaching donors and voters drive many candidates to inconsistently represent their values, the needs of their party, and the will of their constituents.

The Influence of Political Parties Over Time 🔵

Before the mid-20th century, Americans strongly identified with political parties. However, in the last 40 to 50 years, Americans have begun to stray away from party politics, identifying more frequently as independents.

U.S. Party Identification, Yearly Averages, 1988–2016

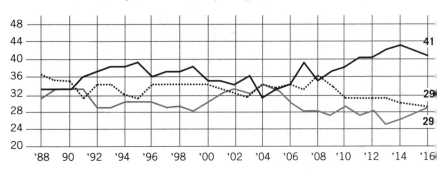

Political candidates have adapted to this new reality in different ways:

- Candidates are less beholden to party doctrine, and are more willing to express their own beliefs on the campaign trail.
- Candidates rely on the advice of trusted political consultants rather than that of party operatives.

"Grassroots" Politics

As the name implies, grassroots politics refers to politics that works from the bottom up. Rather than receive orders from a national party, grassroots movements rely on the support of enthusiastic individuals working toward a common goal.

One of the earliest (and most influential) grassroots politicians in American history was Eugene V. Debs. In the early 20th century, Debs led America's Socialist movement. Able to rally supporters with his expert oratory, he received 6% of the popular vote in the 1912 presidential election.

Today, grassroots politicians use modern technology (e.g., social media) to reach out to and engage with voters, rather than relying on less-immediate forms of communication, like mailers.

"Red States" vs. "Blue States"

Regional differences often arise from different economic and social interests. The major cities and coasts, which are often ethnically and racially mixed, are classified as the country's most liberal regions. Meanwhile, the South and the rural heartland are considered to be more religious and conservative.

With the rise of cable news in the 1980s, political commentators began to discuss the difference between America's "red" (conservative) and "blue" (liberal) states. This is a bit of an oversimplification, but it's one that dominates media coverage.

"The pundits like to slice-and-dice our country into Red States and Blue States; Red States for Republicans, Blue States for Democrats. But I've got news for them, too: We worship an awesome God in the Blue States, and we don't like federal agents poking around in our libraries in the Red States. We coach Little League in the Blue States, and, yes, we've got some gay friends in the Red States."

—Then-U.S. Senatorial Candidate Barack Obama,
at the Democratic National Convention, 2004

Development and Effects on Political Parties 🔴

Like living organisms, political parties must evolve if they are to survive in America's turbulent, cultural ecosystem. As a result, those that have lasted have also evolved due to outside forces.

 Debs Fun Fact: Debs ran his last presidential campaign in 1920 while imprisoned for sedition. His supporters wore buttons proclaiming "For President: Convict No. 9653."

The Deep Roots of American Political Parties ❶

American political parties go back to the late 1780s, when Americans were debating the merits of the then-proposed Constitution. The Federalists, led by Alexander Hamilton, argued for a strong centralized government that chartered a bank to manage an industrialized national economy. The Anti-Federalists, led by Thomas Jefferson, wanted governing power to stay at the state and community level, and the economy to be comprised of small independent farmers. In the timeline below, review how the ideological battle between the Federalists and Anti-Federalists influenced American politics up until the Civil War.

The Anti-Federalist Party

1787 — Various authors including Patrick Henry begin writing *The Anti-Federalist Papers,* a loose series of essays advocating for a weaker central government and the inclusion of a Bill of Rights in the Constitution.

1791 — Thomas Jefferson founds the Democratic-Republican Party based on Anti-Federalist beliefs. Democratic-Republicans control the majority of House/Senate seats from 1800 to 1820.

1800 — The election of Thomas Jefferson begins nearly 30 years of Democratic-Republicans controlling the presidency.

1816–1825 — The "Era of Good Feelings" begins with the end of the War works toward national unity and the abolition

CONTINUED ON NEXT SPREAD BY THE DEMOCRATIC PARTY

The Federalist Party

1787
Alexander Hamilton, John Jay, and James Madison advocate for a strong central government, Bank of the United States, and the Constitution in *The Federalist Papers.*

1789
Alexander Hamilton founds the Federalist Party, the first American political party. Federalists control the majority of House/Senate seats until 1800.

1797
John Adams becomes the first president affiliated with a political party, the Federalists.

1814
The Federalist Party is severely weakened due to its opposition to the War of 1812.

of 1812. Both political parties fray as President James Monroe of political parties.

CONTINUED ON NEXT SPREAD BY THE WHIG PARTY

The Democratic Party

1828

The Democratic Party is formed from members of the dissolved Democratic-Republican Party. The party's platform of small government appeals to rural voters. Until the Civil War, the Democrats are regarded as the nation's pro-slavery party.

1829

Andrew Jackson becomes the first Democratic president.

1850s

Slavery becomes an increasingly divisive issue for the Democratic Party. Northern Democrats, led by Stephen Douglas, argue for abolition or containment of slavery. Southern Democrats, led by Jefferson Davis, argue for continuing slavery throughout southern states.

1860s

The Democratic presidential convention yields two nominees: Stephen Douglas for the Northern Democrats, and John C. Breckenridge for Southern Democrats.

The Whig Party

1824
The Whig Party formed as successor to the dissolved Federalist Party. The Whigs appeal to the country's growing middle class.

1828
Whigs position themselves as the opposition party to the Democrats.

1841
William Henry Harrison becomes the first Whig president. However, he dies a month into his term.

The Republican Party

1854
The Republican Party is founded by followers of the dissolved Whig Party. In addition to adopting many Whig policies, Republicans advocate to "contain" slavery in the South.

1860
Abraham Lincoln is elected the first Republican president. His party's views on slavery prompt the succession movement in the southern United States.

Realignment 🛈

Don't be fooled: just because two parties have dominated U.S. politics for over 150 years does not mean that their political ideologies have been consistent. For example, though the Democratic Party supported slavery in the South leading toward the Civil War, by the 1960s they passed key civil rights legislation as part of the Civil Rights Movement, attracting millions of African American voters who had traditionally supported the Republican Party. As a result, rural whites, traditionally Democratic voters, shifted allegiance to the Republican Party, due in part to the Democratic Party's new stance on civil rights and integration.

Third Parties 💬

Since the Civil War, the Democratic and Republican parties have dominated American politics. Even so, a number of third parties have gone on to influence American politics.

Party Name	Years Active	Reason for Founding	Influence	Reason(s) for Decline
Free Soil Party	1848– 1854	Former members of the Whig party were against the expansion of slavery into the western United States.	Was able to elect two senators and fourteen representatives to Congress.	Joined with former Whigs in 1854 to form the Republican Party.
Populist Party	1891– 1908	Rural farmers felt betrayed by "elites" who suppressed agricultural prices and charged high interest on bank loans.	Impacted the policies of the Democratic Party.	Unable to win national elections. Absorbed by the Democrats.
Progressive (Bull Moose) Party	1912– 1916	Former President Roosevelt believed the United States was not doing enough to implement progressive policies.	Roosevelt won 27% of the popular vote in the 1912 presidential election.	Defeat in many elections weakened the party. Republicans blamed the party for Democratic candidate Woodrow Wilson winning the 1912 presidential election.
Communist Party of the United States	1919– Present	Grew out of America's Socialist Party. Inspired by the success of the 1917 Russian Revolution	Participated in the founding of many workers' unions. Fought against racial segregation.	The Smith Act (1940) banned all political parties that advocate overthrowing the government. In addition, revelations of Soviet atrocities under Stalin severely weakened the party.

Party Name	Years Active	Reason for Founding	Influence	Reason(s) for Decline
American Independent Party	1967–1976	The party was a reaction against the tide of desegregation in the 1950s/1960s.	Governor George Wallace, the party's presidential candidate in 1968, won five southern states.	The party split in 1976. Its successor parties continue to support far-right candidates.
Reform Party	1995–Present	Founded by 1992 presidential candidate Ross Perot. The party attracts voters who believe that the Democratic and Republican parties are unable to govern effectively.	In its most significant victory, former wrestler Jesse Ventura was elected governor of Minnesota in 1998.	Since 2000, the party has been unable to field presidential candidates who receive more than 1% of the popular vote.

| Green Party | 2001– Present | Like the reform party, the "Greens" formed themselves as an alternative to major political parties. Their platform embraces many left-wing beliefs such as progressivism, environmental preservation, and civil rights. | The Greens have won some local and state-level elections; some have argued that Ralph Nader's 2000 presidential run may have sapped crucial votes from the Democratic party. | The party, though still active nationally, has never had a candidate win a U.S. House or Senate seat. |

Effects on the Political Process

Political parties have made a tremendous impact on not only the political process but also on some major events in American history. U.S. politics serves as a valuable mirror for revealing the mood, concerns, and changing cultural beliefs of its citizens.

Politics Shapes American History (and Vice Versa) 💬

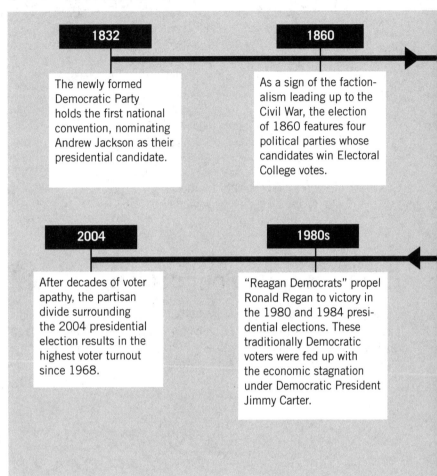

1832

The newly formed Democratic Party holds the first national convention, nominating Andrew Jackson as their presidential candidate.

1860

As a sign of the factionalism leading up to the Civil War, the election of 1860 features four political parties whose candidates win Electoral College votes.

2004

After decades of voter apathy, the partisan divide surrounding the 2004 presidential election results in the highest voter turnout since 1968.

1980s

"Reagan Democrats" propel Ronald Regan to victory in the 1980 and 1984 presidential elections. These traditionally Democratic voters were fed up with the economic stagnation under Democratic President Jimmy Carter.

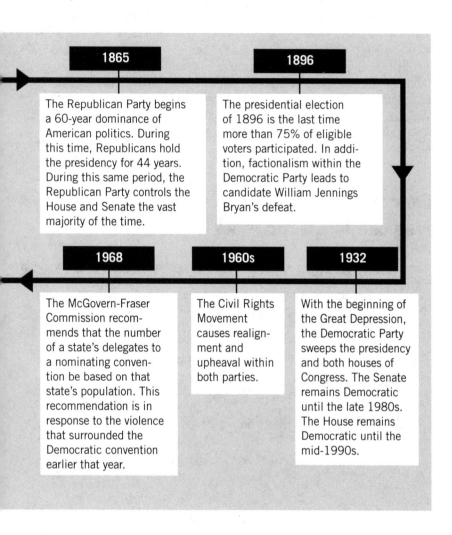

1865

The Republican Party begins a 60-year dominance of American politics. During this time, Republicans hold the presidency for 44 years. During this same period, the Republican Party controls the House and Senate the vast majority of the time.

1896

The presidential election of 1896 is the last time more than 75% of eligible voters participated. In addition, factionalism within the Democratic Party leads to candidate William Jennings Bryan's defeat.

1968

The McGovern-Fraser Commission recommends that the number of a state's delegates to a nominating convention be based on that state's population. This recommendation is in response to the violence that surrounded the Democratic convention earlier that year.

1960s

The Civil Rights Movement causes realignment and upheaval within both parties.

1932

With the beginning of the Great Depression, the Democratic Party sweeps the presidency and both houses of Congress. The Senate remains Democratic until the late 1980s. The House remains Democratic until the mid-1990s.

 Ask Yourself...

Write down some of your political beliefs. Based on research into the parties of the 1900s, 1950s, and present day, which parties would you have supported?

Electoral Laws and Systems

General elections for federal office are held on the first Tuesday after the first Monday of November. Elections in which the president is being chosen are called **presidential elections**. These elections, also known as general elections, are preceded by primary elections and caucuses that take place between March and late spring, depending on the state. Those elections that occur between presidential elections are called **midterm elections.**

Congressional Elections vs. Presidential Elections ❗

House Elections	Senate Elections	Presidential Elections
Candidates receive party endorsement after a primary.		
Elected directly by the people every **2 years.**	Elected directly by the people every **6 years.**	Elected by the Electoral College every **4 years.**
District-wide election.	**State-wide election.**	**National election.**
In 2010, **85%** of incumbents won reelection.	In 2010, **84%** of incumbents won reelection.	Out of the 42 presidents who were elected to a first term, only 15 were reelected to a second **(36%).**
Many candidates come from **state legislatures,** though some have no government experience.	Many candidates come from the **House of Representatives.**	Many candidates come from **state governorships and the Senate.**

Types of Congressional and Presidential Primaries 🔟

The majority of states (39) use **primary elections** to select presidential nominees. **All** states use some form of primary election to select legislative and state nominees. These elections are usually held between early February and late spring of an election year. Each state sets its own rules for these elections, and there is considerable variation in primary procedures from state to state. There are three main types of primaries.

Types of Congressional and Presidential Primaries

Closed Primary

• This most common type restricts voting to registered members of a political party. Voters may vote only for candidates running for the nomination of their declared party.

For example: An Independent cannot vote for a Democratic or Republican candidate.

Open Primary

• Voters may vote only in one party's primary, but they may vote in whichever one they choose. This decision is made from the privacy of the voting booth.

For example: A democrat can vote for a Democratic or Republican candidate.

Blanket Primary

• This method uses the same procedure as a general election. Voters may vote for one candidate per office of either party. Only Alaska and Washington state use this primary system.

For example: A Republican can choose among Democratic and Republican candidates.

In primary voting for legislators and state officials, a candidate can win either by receiving a majority (more than half) or a plurality (more than any other candidate) of votes. In a state that requires a winner to receive a minimum percentage of the vote, a **runoff primary** is sometimes held—this is basically a revote, but one in which only the top two candidates are on the ballot. Runoffs occur most often when many challengers vie for an open office, especially when none of them are well known.

The Presidential Primary and Caucus Systems !

The process by which political parties select their presidential candidate begins at the state level.

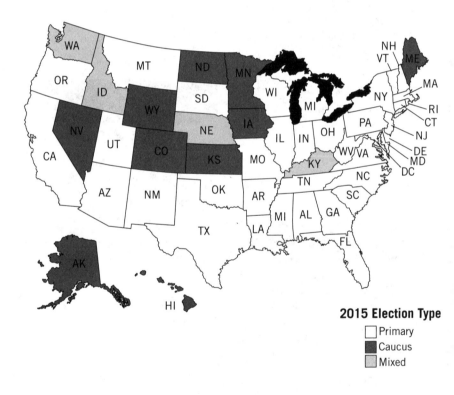

2015 Election Type
- ☐ Primary
- ■ Caucus
- ▨ Mixed

☐ Many states hold **primary elections,** in which voters select their desired candidate and the delegate who will represent them at the national convention.

■ Other states select a presidential candidate and convention delegates at **state caucuses** and **conventions**. This process begins with local meetings of party members, who select representatives to send to statewide party meetings. Compared with primaries, the state caucus and convention process usually attracts fewer participants, most of whom are more politically active and better informed than typical voters.

▨ Four states utilize a combination of both methods.

 The television show *Survivor* comes down to runoff voting whenever there's a tie between two contestants. Maybe *that's* why they call it reality TV!

Other Convention Voters

The Democratic Party reserves a privileged status at its national convention for elected party leaders such as congresspersons and important state leaders. Known as **superdelegates,** these individuals also get to cast a vote for their party's presidential candidate. The Republicans have a less formal and more restrictive method:

Democrat
- The superdelegate retains the right to vote for the candidate of his or her choice.

Republican
- Three extra people get to vote per state, but these members are bound to vote according to the outcome of the primary election or caucus in their state.

Critics complain that the superdelegates dilute the importance of the primary elections by making it easier for the party elite to control the nominating process.

The Primary Schedule

- New Hampshire holds the first presidential primary.
- Iowa holds the first presidential caucus.
- The first primaries and caucuses create frontloading, forcing candidates to win early, or not at all. Voters criticize this process because it "trims away" many candidates before voters in other states cast their ballots or caucus.
  - Early primaries/caucuses provide a boost of media and fund-raising support to the winners.
  - Major donors abandon poorly performing candidates.
  - Voters often have to choose early on, before they've gotten to know the candidates well, which often favors those who are already familiar to voters.
- If a candidate receives less than 10% of the vote in two successive primaries, he or she loses federal matching funds.
- Super Tuesday is the first Tuesday in March when many states have their primaries. Traditionally, it is on Super Tuesday when the parties' nominees become clear.

- Primaries and caucuses continue into late spring, but a victor is usually decided well before that point.
  - Some larger states such as New York and California have moved their primary dates earlier in the year in the hopes of having a greater influence on which candidates win the nomination.

National Conventions ❗

After the primary season has ended, both parties hold **national conventions** to confirm their nominee. When no candidate has received the pledge of a majority of convention delegates, conventions choose the nominee through **brokered conventions**. With the adoption of primary elections in the 20th century, conventions have been transformed into mere coronations with the nominees generally being determined long before the conventions begin.

One of the main purposes of a modern national convention is to unify the party after a hard primary battle. Conventions also make a show of party unity for political gain. Both parties' conventions are nationally televised and are widely covered by the media.

Conventions are the site of many political negotiations, as well; different factions of the party attempt to win concessions in return for their full support during the general election.

Conventions usually help their candidates considerably. Polls taken immediately after conventions show an increase in candidates' approval ratings. This rise in public approval is called a post-convention bump.

 The comedian Stephen Colbert used to encourage politicians (and celebrities) to appear on his show because they'd get the so-called "Colbert bump." We encourage you to use this book in the hopes that it'll bump up your scores on the AP Exam!

The General Election and the Electoral College ❗

Once the parties choose their candidates, the candidates continue to campaign for the general election in much the same way as they campaigned during the primaries: holding rallies, participating in debates, running campaign advertisements, and pursuing positive media coverage.

Key Differences between Primary and General Elections ❗

Primary Election
- Candidates run against members of their own party.
- Prmary elections focus on generally subtle differences between how the candidates approach the party's platform (central beliefs).
- This is a time to "court the base" with rhetoric that appeals to partisan members of the party who are likely to vote in primary elections.

General Election
- Candidates run against members of other parties.
- General elections focus on general policy and philosophical differences between the two parties.
- This is a time to "court the nation" with rhetoric that appeals to Americans with more moderate political beliefs.

Electoral College

Candidates planning their campaign strategies must consider the nature of the Electoral College, an institution created by the framers of the Constitution as a means of insulating the government from the whims of a less-educated public.

- Each state gets a number of electors that is equal to the sum of their federal legislators—two senators and a number of House representatives proportional to their population.

- Of the 538 Electoral College votes available, a candidate needs 270 to win.

- The most populous states, like California (55) or Texas (38), are worth the most, which is why so many resources are put into winning those states.

- Winning New York by a single popular vote gets you all 29 electoral votes. Doing the same in Vermont gets you only 3.

- Candidates also focus on swing states, areas in which polling indicates a close race.

- Special emphasis also goes to those states that hold the earliest primaries, like Iowa, because success in those states can build momentum and name-recognition for that candidate in other states.

Critics feel the Electoral College system is antiquated, but no one has yet successfully proposed an amendment to change it.

To win an Electoral College majority, candidates devise strategies when planning their campaigns. In 1968, Republican Richard Nixon campaigned heavily in the South, a traditionally Democratic stronghold. Nixon's "Southern strategy" swung the election to Republicans.

Winner Take All 💬

The **winner-take-all** system of the Electoral College distorts the results of the popular vote. In 1992, Ross Perot received 19% of the popular vote but 0 electoral votes. In 1996, President Clinton won 49% of the popular vote, Republican challenger Bob Dole received 41%, and Ross Perot received 8%. In the electoral college, however, Clinton won 70%, Dole 30%, and Perot 0%. The discrepancy was also apparent in 2000.

	% of Popular Vote	Electoral Vote	% of Electoral Vote
Gore	48.38	267	49.63
Bush	47.87	271	50.37
Nader	.42	0	0
Buchanan	2.74	0	0

The election of 2000 was one of the closest in American history. It was unusual because the winner of the popular vote lost the election in the Electoral College. A difference of 400 to 500 popular votes in Florida would have given the election to Gore because he would have received all of Florida's electoral votes. As it turned out, Bush won the presidency by the minimum number of electoral votes possible, with Gore winning the national popular vote. Similar events occurred in 2016, when Donald Trump won the election with 306 Electoral College votes, though he won only 46.4% of the popular vote.

Bush v. Gore (2000)

The contest between Bush and Gore was so close that the Florida Supreme Court ordered a manual recount of votes in select counties in the greater Miami area, as Florida was a critical swing state in the election. The U.S. Supreme Court ruled that the recount violated the Equal Protection clause of the Fourteenth Amendment because it subjected votes to "later arbitrary and disparate treatment," and that the state Supreme Court lacked the authority to define election procedures. As a result, Bush won the Electoral College with 271 votes to Gore's 266 despite having lost the popular vote.

Interest Groups & PACs 🗯️

For every position a politician can take, there is an interest group or political action committee (PAC) that exists to support or oppose it at the local, state, and national level. These groups spend billions of dollars to influence voters and politicians. In many cases, the support of an interest group can propel a campaign to victory; the opposite can sink it.

Interest Groups Explored 🗯️

Washington, D.C. is home to approximately 13,500 registered lobbyists. This number translates to 25 lobbyists for each member of Congress. These lobbyists represent a wide range of interest groups.

Type of Interest Group	Purpose	Examples
Labor Unions	Promote the rights of workers in different industries.	• American Federation of Labor–Congress of Industrial Organizations (AFL-CIO) • National Education Association (NEA)
Racial	Fight for social and legal equality between different racial groups.	• National Association for the Advancement of Colored People (NAACP) • Rainbow/PUSH Coalition
Environmental	Preserve the environmental quality of the nation's water, air, and land.	• Sierra Club
Business	Expand opportunities for American businesses both at home and abroad.	• U.S. Chamber of Commerce • National Association of Manufacturers
Professional	Advocate for the members of a specific profession.	• American Medical Association (AMA)

Type of Interest Group	Purpose	Examples
Single-Issue	Fight for or against "hot button" issues such as abortion or gun control.	• National Rifle Association (NRA) • National Organization for Women (NOW) • Christian Coalition
Consumer Public Interest	Protect consumers against fraud.	• Better Business Bureau (BBB)

The Relationship Between 527s and Interest Groups

In their 1976 ruling on *Buckley v. Valeo*, the Supreme Court struck down limits on campaign spending, declaring them a violation of the First Amendment's right to free speech. Interest groups took advantage of this to extend their influence, filing with the IRS as "527 organizations." As a 527, an interest group is tax-exempt, which more easily allows them to raise and spend millions of dollars on political advertisements. Their one stipulation is that they must not endorse a specific candidate; they can, however, attack other candidates on "issues."

What Interest Groups Do

Interest groups perform many of the same functions as political parties. In the schedule below, review the workings of interest groups through the eyes of a single Washington, D.C. lobbyist.

9:00–10:00 AM:
Meeting with Congressman Smith about proposed legislation.

Lobbyists routinely meet with members of Congress to educate them on issues and advocate their interest group's point of view.

10:15–11:30 AM:
Phone calls with NYC donors.

Lobbyists are always raising money to fund their interest groups.

11:45 AM–12:15 PM:
Lunch with Senator Green.

Lobbyists treat members of Congress to lunch or dinner. Lobbyists continue to advocate for their positions in these less-formal settings.

12:30–1:30 PM:
Edit testimony for Friday.

Lobbyists give testimony to Congress, acting as the mouthpiece for the interest groups they represent.

1:45–2:45 PM:
Make endorsement recommendations.

Like political parties, interest groups endorse candidates for office. Lobbyists participate in electioneering, actively working to influence voters during election season.

3:00–4:00 PM:
Begin writing amicus brief.

Amicus curiae briefs, a holdover from English law, are informative pieces meant to sway the Supreme Court. For example, the NAACP submitted an amicus brief before the Court ruled on Brown v. The Board of Education.

4:15–5:00 PM:
Grassroots brainstorming session with staff.

Interest groups are always exploring new ways to rally their supporters to take action on their behalf. Some members of Congress are more likely to be persuaded through the opinions of voters rather than direct lobbying.

5:15–6:00 PM:
Review final draft of press release.

Interest groups (527 or not) spend much of their money on advertisements, mailers, and press releases.

Interest groups often assign "grades" to members of Congress based on their voting history. In attempting to unseat a member of Congress who supports gun control, the NRA will send out mailers featuring a picture of that member next to a large red F.

Regulation of Interest Groups ❗

Since the 1940s, the federal government has taken action to regulate interest groups. In the last few years, however, it has become easier than ever for interest groups to influence elections.

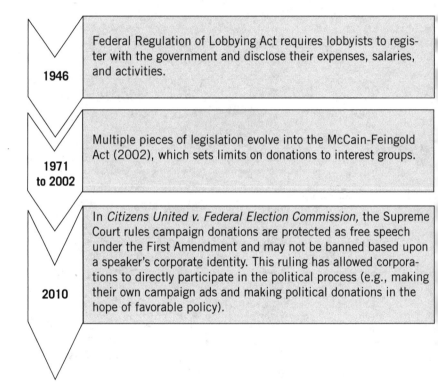

1946 — Federal Regulation of Lobbying Act requires lobbyists to register with the government and disclose their expenses, salaries, and activities.

1971 to 2002 — Multiple pieces of legislation evolve into the McCain-Feingold Act (2002), which sets limits on donations to interest groups.

2010 — In *Citizens United v. Federal Election Commission,* the Supreme Court rules campaign donations are protected as free speech under the First Amendment and may not be banned based upon a speaker's corporate identity. This ruling has allowed corporations to directly participate in the political process (e.g., making their own campaign ads and making political donations in the hope of favorable policy).

Though interest groups themselves are stronger than ever, Congress still has regulations on its members becoming lobbyists after leaving office. Members of Congress must wait a year after leaving Congress before registering as lobbyists. For members of the executive branch, the wait is even longer. Despite these rules, Congress is still regarded as a "revolving door" to the more lucrative lobbying industry.

 Ask Yourself...

1. Do you agree with the decision in *Citizens United?* Is a financial donation the equivalent of free speech? Are corporations entitled to rights protected by the First Amendment? Why or why not?

2. Why are certain segments of the population able to exert pressures on political institutions and actors in order to obtain favorable policies, while others are not?

PACs & Super PACs 💬

As of 1974, corporations, unions, trade organizations, and other special interest groups have been able to form political action committees (PACs) to raise money and support political campaigns and causes. **PACs have become a key means through which interest groups influence elections,** as candidates face huge pressure to raise money given the increasing costs associated with running for office (in 2016, the average elected senator spent $10.4 million dollars to win; Senator Pat Toomey's campaign spent $27.8 million to keep his Pennsylvania seat).

There are limits to how much a PAC can spend:

- Only $5,000 per candidate per election
- Only $15,000 per political party per year

In 2010, in the wake of the *Citizens United* decision, **Super PACs** began to form. Super PACs are unique in that they aren't associated with a specific candidate or party, so there are no limits to the amount of money a Super PAC can spend to support a cause. For example, a Super PAC may fund attack ads to run against the opponent of a candidate who supports favorable policy for the Super PAC. Super PACs are criticized as being undemocratic as donors are often kept secret and politicians are vulnerable to corruption given the high cost of elections. Arguments in favor of campaign finance reform often hinge on limiting the contributions of Super PACs.

"We have the best government that money can buy."
—Mark Twain

Mass Media 🔞

Also known as the "fourth estate" or seen as a fourth branch of government, the mass media plays a vital role in the American political process. Whether it's from a series of long-form articles in print newspapers or an up-to-the-minute tweet, Americans are awash in news 24/7. With so much exposure, it is no surprise that the mass media influences American's political beliefs.

The History of Mass Media in the United States 🔞

The concept of mass media took off in the mid to late 19th century, thanks to inventions such as the telegraph and telephone, which allowed news to travel at the speed of light. In the combined set of three timelines on the following page, you can see how each type of media has evolved to provide Americans with the news.

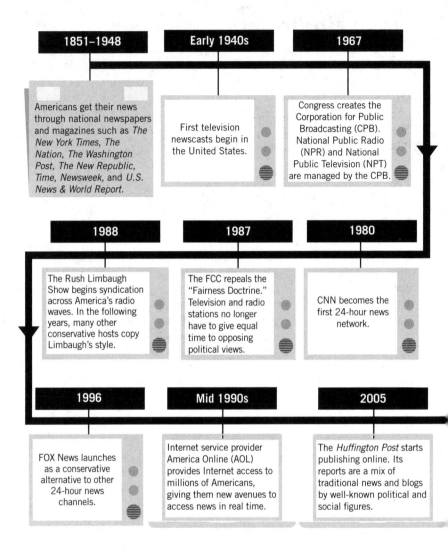

1851–1948

Americans get their news through national newspapers and magazines such as *The New York Times, The Nation, The Washington Post, The New Republic, Time, Newsweek,* and *U.S. News & World Report.*

Early 1940s

First television newscasts begin in the United States.

1967

Congress creates the Corporation for Public Broadcasting (CPB). National Public Radio (NPR) and National Public Television (NPT) are managed by the CPB.

1988

The Rush Limbaugh Show begins syndication across America's radio waves. In the following years, many other conservative hosts copy Limbaugh's style.

1987

The FCC repeals the "Fairness Doctrine." Television and radio stations no longer have to give equal time to opposing political views.

1980

CNN becomes the first 24-hour news network.

1996

FOX News launches as a conservative alternative to other 24-hour news channels.

Mid 1990s

Internet service provider America Online (AOL) provides Internet access to millions of Americans, giving them new avenues to access news in real time.

2005

The *Huffington Post* starts publishing online. Its reports are a mix of traditional news and blogs by well-known political and social figures.

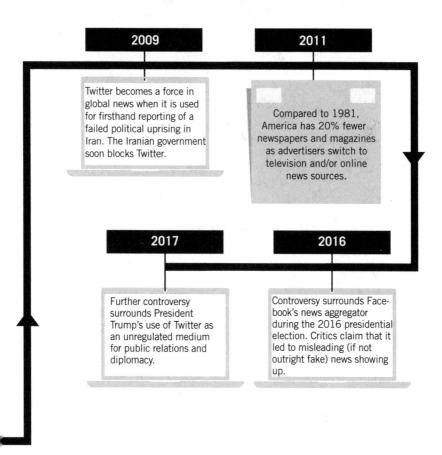

2009

Twitter becomes a force in global news when it is used for firsthand reporting of a failed political uprising in Iran. The Iranian government soon blocks Twitter.

2011

Compared to 1981, America has 20% fewer newspapers and magazines as advertisers switch to television and/or online news sources.

2017

Further controversy surrounds President Trump's use of Twitter as an unregulated medium for public relations and diplomacy.

2016

Controversy surrounds Facebook's news aggregator during the 2016 presidential election. Critics claim that it led to misleading (if not outright fake) news showing up.

The News Media "Industry" ❶

Many argue that the consolidation/industrialization of the news has put the mass media's power in too few hands. The Walt Disney Company, for example, entertains millions of people every day with its films, television shows, and theme parks. But through ABC, a subsidiary, Disney also has the opportunity to inform Americans during the nightly news. Disney and four other companies (Comcast, 21st Century Fox, Time Warner, and National Amusements) control 90% of the broadcast media in the United States.

As television and the Internet changed mass media, corporations began buying struggling newspapers and smaller media outlets. From 1983 to today, the number of companies controlling America's mass media dropped from 50 to only 6. This is a critical change, as the mass media plays an important role in any functioning democracy: to continually scrutinize the actions of the government, providing citizens with impartial information they can use to make social and political choices in their best interest. With fewer companies controlling the news, there are fewer entities regulating the government.

As a result, in recent years Americans have been getting their news from fewer sources. Further, the bias of media outlets has increased after the abolition of the Fairness Doctrine. Traditionally, a newspaper might print the entirety of a president's speech; today, a media outlet might feature only sound bites taken out of context and analysis geared to persuading the audience toward a certain perspective. Additionally, that same outlet may run only political ads representing a similar view. As a result, there has been an increase in skepticism about the accuracy and completeness of the news, and this has degraded trustworthiness to the point at which once reliable news outlets are now being accused of reporting "fake news." In fact, many attribute the lack of unbiased news reporting in America as one of the causes of the national divisiveness apparent in the 2016 election.

Mass Media's Impact on Politics ❗

Impact	Effect
Gatekeeping / Agenda Setting	Media outlets often influence America's political conversations and politicians' actions/positions. This happens because the media choose which topics to cover, and for how long.
"Horse race" Journalism	Media outlets provide easily digestible information (such as candidates' polling numbers) rather than their complex political views. This happens because the primary concern of a media outlet is its number of viewers/listeners/subscribers.
Televised Presidential Debates	Though political debates have a long tradition in American history, the age of television changed the game forever. Regarding the first televised debates in the 1960s, many argue that Kennedy's good looks vs. Nixon's haggard appearance (Nixon was recovering from a severe infection) swung crucial votes to Kennedy and won him the presidential election.
Spin	"Spin" is a form of propaganda used to influence media consumers' political beliefs. Media outlets may produce their own spin in the form of biased newscasts, or allow time to political professionals whose job it is to spin a story a particular way.

In the 1976 film *Network*, a reporter laments the power given over to the television: "This tube is the most awesome ... propaganda force in the whole ... world, and woe is us if it ever falls into the hands of the wrong people." Go ahead and pat yourself on the back if you've never been fooled by something on TV.

When Politicians Circumvent the Media

The media provide Americans with a picture of politicians and their beliefs, although this viewpoint may change depending on the organization's agenda. Some politicians choose to avoid media bias entirely and reach voters directly. President Roosevelt used the radio to broadcast over 30 "fireside chats": radio conversations with the American people. In these addresses, he discussed his New Deal programs.

In today's political landscape, most government officials have access to official social media accounts, which they can use to quickly react to or get ahead of the news. Elected officials can also directly reach out to voters through televised addresses, books, and editorials in major news outlets.

 Ask Yourself...

In the relationship between the mass media and politicians, who is the most powerful partner?

How Politicians Manipulate the Media

President Ronald Reagan's former career as an actor gave him the charm and charisma he needed to win over the media during his two presidential campaigns. In the decades since, politicians have attempted to mimic Reagan. For example, politicians may go on certain television shows to win over the youth vote. Others may stage elaborate campaign events.

Nowadays, the president has a team—the press corps—on hand to help maintain a specific image. This group, which includes official photographers, interacts with the media and limits its access to the president. At the head of this group is the White House Press Secretary, who holds almost daily conferences that are designed to release an official, unified message to the press.

 The Press Secretary's job is so straightforward that *SNL* got a lot of mileage out of Melissa McCarthy's comic portrayal of a press secretary who is seemingly incapable of being forthright.

CHAPTER 4

The Congress, the Presidency, the Bureaucracy, and the Federal Courts

The federal government has three branches: the Congress, the presidency, and the federal court system. The bureaucracy, though not an official government branch, is essential because its 2.7 million employees execute the government's will. This chapter reviews each branch, and how they work together.

The Congress 〽️

Congress is a bicameral (two-house) legislature: the Senate and the House of Representatives. Each body has a different power and number of members, but only together can they write and pass legislation.

Congress: The Bare Essentials 〽️

The two chambers of Congress are like two houses. They serve a similar purpose, but are unique in their own special ways.

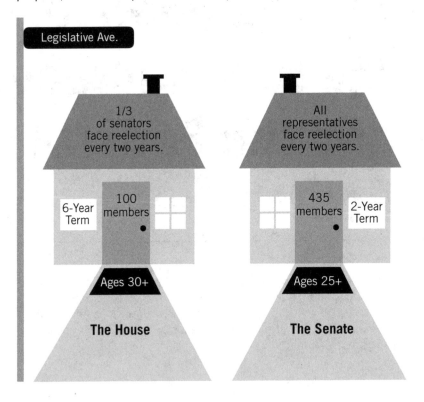

Legislative Ave.

1/3 of senators face reelection every two years.

All representatives face reelection every two years.

6-Year Term | 100 members | 2-Year Term | 435 members

Ages 30+

Ages 25+

The House

The Senate

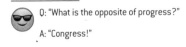

Q: "What is the opposite of progress?"

A: "Congress!"

If a 51st state ever joins the United States, that state will send two senators to the Senate, making the total number of senators 102. However, there can be no more seats added to the House. For the new state to gain its share of seats, other states would have to give up some of theirs, a process known as congressional reapportionment.

 Ask Yourself...

Why do the Senate and the House have different age requirements?

How is Congress Elected?

The Senate

- Before the 17th Amendment (1913), senators were chosen by state legislatures. They are now elected by the popular vote of their constituents.

The House

- Within a congressional district, the winner of that district's popular vote becomes the next representative.
- Although Congress reapportions the number of House seats granted to each state after every national census, state legislatures choose how to draw their own congressional districts.
- For most of American history, state legislatures have used **gerry-mandering,** redrawing congressional districts to favor the political party in power.

 Ask Yourself...

Just by looking at a map of congressional districts, how might you tell that a district was gerrymandered?

Congressional Powers ❗

The Constitution grants certain powers to Congress. These powers are described in Article I, Section 8.

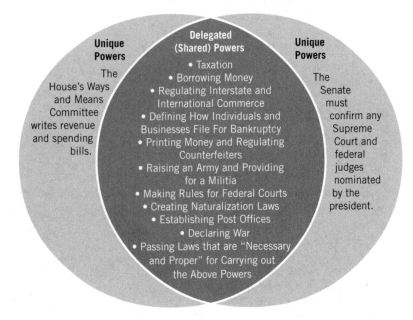

Unique Powers

The House's Ways and Means Committee writes revenue and spending bills.

Delegated (Shared) Powers

- Taxation
- Borrowing Money
- Regulating Interstate and International Commerce
- Defining How Individuals and Businesses File For Bankruptcy
- Printing Money and Regulating Counterfeiters
- Raising an Army and Providing for a Militia
- Making Rules for Federal Courts
- Creating Naturalization Laws
- Establishing Post Offices
- Declaring War
- Passing Laws that are "Necessary and Proper" for Carrying out the Above Powers

Unique Powers

The Senate must confirm any Supreme Court and federal judges nominated by the president.

Throughout U.S. history, Congress has gained further powers relating to spending. The Budget and Impoundment Control Act (1974) gave Congress the power to stop the president from impounding (withholding) funds from programs that the president did not like.

Army v. Militia 💬

The framers of the Constitution felt the need to distinguish between an "army" and a "militia" due to their experience leading up to the Revolutionary War. The framers worried that by maintaining an army of professional soldiers led by highly trained elite officers, like the British did in the colonies, the American government would pose a threat to individual freedoms. Further, they viewed the capacity for all citizens to unite in armed conflict as required for maintaining personal liberty (thus the Second Amendment). As a result, the Constitution distinguishes how and when the Congress may raise an army comprised of professional soldiers, as opposed to how and when they may raise a militia comprised of citizen soldiers (in modern terms, this is the National Guard).

Members of Congress think of themselves as either **trustees** or **delegates** of the people who elected them. Trustees exercise their own judgment when making important decisions such as how to vote on bills. Delegates, on the other hand, strictly follow their constituents' wishes.

Congress's Other Tasks 🛑

Besides writing legislation and casting votes, Congress performs many nonlegislative tasks.

- Through committees and subcommittees, Congress reviews the work of the federal government. If they suspect wrongdoing, they can subpoena witnesses and hear testimony.
- As congressional debates are open to the public and press, debates educate citizens on important issues facing the nation.
- Members of Congress regularly help their constituents. Much of this help comes in the form of improving the relationship between the senator's state (or representative's district) and the federal government. When visiting their home states or districts, members of Congress routinely meet with constituents to hear constituents' problems or concerns.

Restrictions on Congress 🛑

Congress may have a lot of power, but that doesn't mean the Constitution doesn't restrict what Congress can do.

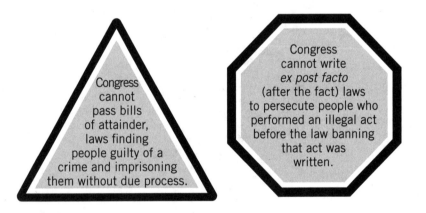

Congress cannot pass bills of attainder, laws finding people guilty of a crime and imprisoning them without due process.

Congress cannot write *ex post facto* (after the fact) laws to persecute people who performed an illegal act before the law banning that act was written.

Impeachment !

Congress has the power to impeach and remove federal officials who commit "treason, bribery, and other high crimes and misdemeanors." Impeachments are rare, and are handled in the following fashion.

A member of the House begins impeachment proceedings by submitting a resolution, much like he or she would submit a bill.

The resolution goes to the House Committee on the Judiciary for debate.

The House votes on impeachment.

If one or more articles of impeachment passes by a simple majority, the Senate holds a trial similar to a jury trial. The accused can mount a defense and have his or her own lawyers present. The Chief Justice of the Supreme Court presides over the trial.

If 2/3 of senators vote to convict, the accused is immediately removed from office. The accused may also face criminal prosecution for his or her crimes. If fewer than 2/3 of senators vote to convict, the accused remains in office.

America's 2.5 Presidential Impeachments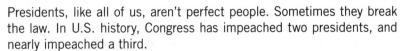

Presidents, like all of us, aren't perfect people. Sometimes they break the law. In U.S. history, Congress has impeached two presidents, and nearly impeached a third.

The Years: 1867–1868

The Accused: President Andrew Johnson (Democrat)

The Crime: Firing the Secretary of War without congressional approval.

Impeached by the House? Impeached

Convicted by the Senate? Acquitted by a single vote.

The Years: 1972–1974

The Accused: President Richard Nixon (Republican)

The Crime: Obstructing justice in an attempt to cover up the break-in of the Democrat National Committee at the Watergate complex.

Impeached by the House? He may very well have been, but Nixon resigned before the House could do so. He received a pardon from his successor, President Gerald Ford.

The Years: 1998–1999

The Accused: President Bill Clinton (Democrat)

The Crime: Perjury and obstruction of justice in an attempt to cover up an extramarital affair.

Impeached by the House? Impeached on two of the four counts brought against him.

Convicted by the Senate? Acquitted on both counts of impeachment.

 Ask Yourself...

Although Republicans in Congress loathed Andrew Johnson, why might have some Republican senators thought that removing Johnson was a bad idea?

 Despite sounding like the succulent summertime fruit, and much to the regret of some politicians, you can't "impeach" a president simply by throwing peaches.

Congressional Leadership ❗

The House and Senate have similar, but not identical, leadership structures.

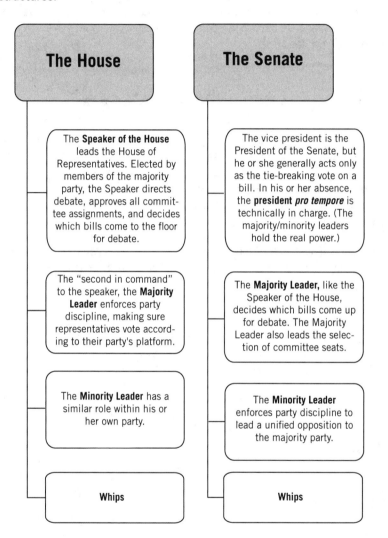

The House

The **Speaker of the House** leads the House of Representatives. Elected by members of the majority party, the Speaker directs debate, approves all committee assignments, and decides which bills come to the floor for debate.

The "second in command" to the speaker, the **Majority Leader** enforces party discipline, making sure representatives vote according to their party's platform.

The **Minority Leader** has a similar role within his or her own party.

Whips

The Senate

The vice president is the President of the Senate, but he or she generally acts only as the tie-breaking vote on a bill. In his or her absence, the **president *pro tempore*** is technically in charge. (The majority/minority leaders hold the real power.)

The **Majority Leader,** like the Speaker of the House, decides which bills come up for debate. The Majority Leader also leads the selection of committee seats.

The **Minority Leader** enforces party discipline to lead a unified opposition to the majority party.

Whips

Whips

Whips are the deputies of the majority and minority leaders, assisting in keeping congressional members in line when it comes to supporting or opposing bills. They do this by tracking how their party members vote on bills. Whips also report the concerns of party members to the majority or minority leaders.

Committees and Subcommittees

Committees and subcommittees are where the bulk of Congress's work happens. Bills are investigated and debated. If a bill is too complex for the entire committee, it is sent to a subcommittee, where it can receive extra attention from an even smaller subset of Congress. Experts testify on bills and witnesses are subpoenaed to provide testimony if the need arises. As a result, the power held by individual members of Congress largely stems from their committee assignments.

Members of Congress in the minority party rarely get their first picks of committee seats. Even so, all new members of Congress put a lot of thought into what committees they want to join.

Types of Committees ❗

Representatives and senators perform their work in one or more kinds of committees.

Type of Committee	Permanent? (Y/N)	# in House/ Senate	Special Features	Examples
Standing committees	Y	20 in the House 17 in the Senate	These specialized groups are the most important committees. Each one has 2 to 12 subcommittees that investigate/review specific topics.	House Ways and Means Committee debates tax bills
Joint committees	Y	5 total	These committees include members of the House and Senate. They rarely deal with legislation. Congress uses them mainly for investigations. **NOTE:** Some joint committees are also also standing committees.	Joint Committee on Taxation
Select committees (a.k.a. ad-hoc committees)	N	Varies at any given time	These temporary committees are created for a special purpose. Historically, the Senate has used these committees to conduct special investigations.	In the early 1970s, the Senate Watergate Committee investigated President Nixon's cover-up of the Watergate break-in.

Type of Committee	Permanent? (Y/N)	# in House/ Senate	Special Features	Examples
Conference Committees	N	Varies at any given time	These committees, which include members of the House and Senate, exist to combine versions of a bill. Once finished, the committee disbands.	In 2016, the Opioids Conference Committee was formed to create a unified bill to combat opioic addiction in America.

Though part of the larger legislative body, representatives serve on fewer committees than senators. Because they spend more time working on fewer issues, representatives have a greater expertise on their committees' topics than senators who serve on similar committees.

 Ask Yourself...

Put yourself in the shoes of several newly elected members of the House of Representatives.

1. I am from a rural state with many farms. On which committee can I help my constituents?
2. Before being elected, I was an engineer. On which committee can I put my skills to use?
3. I want to be a powerful congressperson. On which committee will I have the most influence?

Key Committees

Given the scope of their jurisdiction, a number of key standing committees hold considerable sway over the legislative process.

Committee	Type	What They Do
Rules	Standing, House of Representatives	Determines under what rules a bill will be presented on the floor, including the length of debate proceedings and whether or not new amendments will be allowed
Ways and Means	Standing, House of Representatives	Manages the acquisition of government funds through taxes
Appropriations	Standing, Senate	Determines how the government allocates funds between states, programs, and bureaucracies
Judiciary	Standing, Senate	Conducts hearings and approves or denies presidential appointments to the federal judiciary, including the Supreme Court
Foreign Relations	Standing, Senate	Regulates issues relating to foreign aid, treaties, and weapons sales. Leads all foreign-policy related debate and legislation

How a Bill Becomes a Law: The Board Game! (Suitable for Ages 25–91) 🔋

You are a member of the House who has a great idea for a new law. Your bill is ready to go. Begin by submitting it, but remember that even if your bill makes it through, it still needs to pass through the Senate.

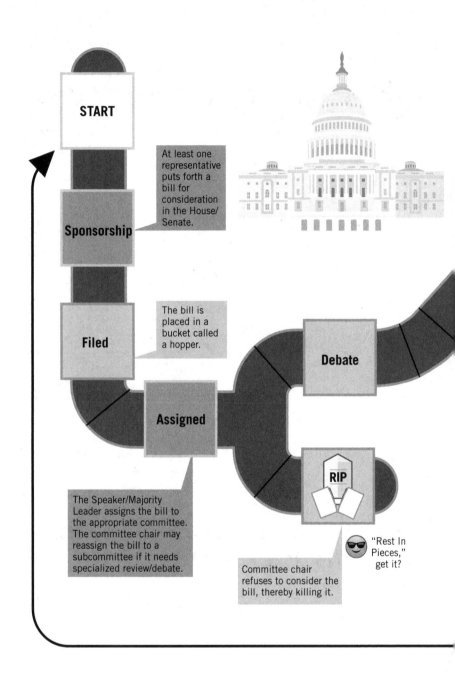

START

Sponsorship

At least one representative puts forth a bill for consideration in the House/Senate.

Filed

The bill is placed in a bucket called a hopper.

Assigned

Debate

RIP

The Speaker/Majority Leader assigns the bill to the appropriate committee. The committee chair may reassign the bill to a subcommittee if it needs specialized review/debate.

Committee chair refuses to consider the bill, thereby killing it.

"Rest In Pieces," get it?

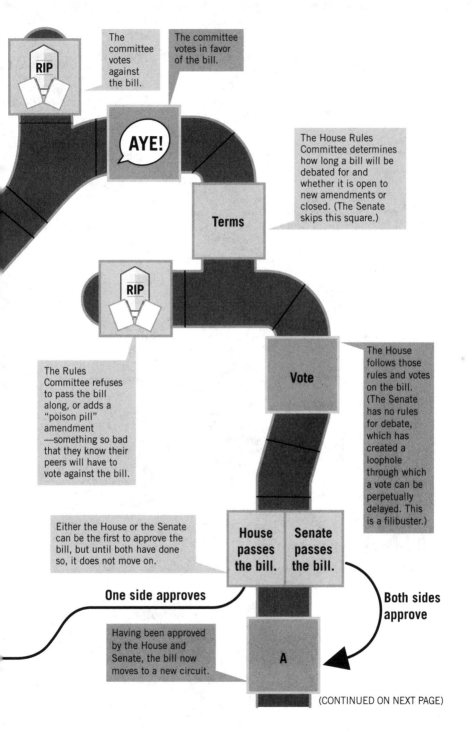

(CONTINUED ON NEXT PAGE)

The Congress, the Presidency, the Bureaucracy, and the Federal Courts   **129**

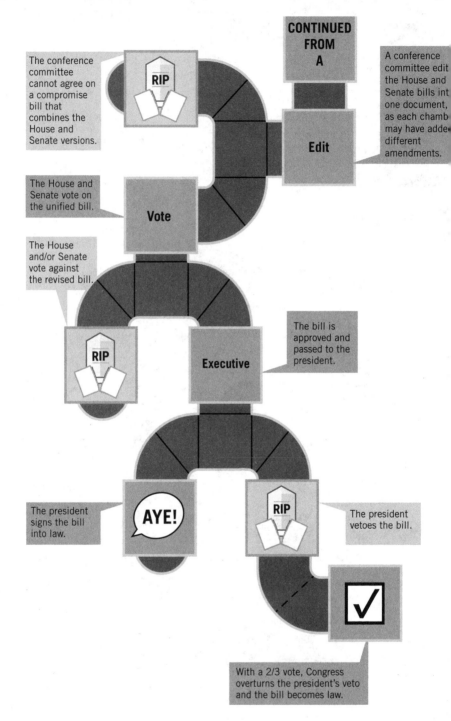

CONTINUED FROM A

The conference committee cannot agree on a compromise bill that combines the House and Senate versions.

RIP

A conference committee edit the House and Senate bills int one document, as each chamb may have adde different amendments.

Edit

The House and Senate vote on the unified bill.

Vote

The House and/or Senate vote against the revised bill.

RIP

The bill is approved and passed to the president.

Executive

The president signs the bill into law.

AYE!

RIP

The president vetoes the bill.

With a 2/3 vote, Congress overturns the president's veto and the bill becomes law.

Filibusters and Cloture

The **filibuster** is a powerful tactic used by the minority party to delay a vote that they suspect they are going to lose. The most commonly employed version is when a senator runs out the clock on a vote by refusing to yield control, an act that usually requires them to continuously address the Senate while standing before them. **Cloture** is the only way to override this act, but it requires 60 members to call for it. The more evenly represented the two parties are, the harder it is to overturn a filibuster.

 Ask Yourself...

How does the process by which a bill becomes a law influence the fact that so few bills become laws?

Watershed Laws

Throughout American history, some of Congress's laws have fundamentally changed the workings of the federal government. The four laws below are only a sample of Congressional action:

Year	Law	Effect
1883	Pendleton Act	Ended the patronage system, wherein less-than-qualified individuals were given government jobs as favors. Applicants now have to pass rigorous tests.
1966	Freedom of Information Act	Created a system by which the public could gain access to once-classified government documents.
1971, 1974	Federal Election Campaign Acts	Created the Federal Election Commission (FEC). The FEC requires that presidential candidates disclose certain financial information such as donations and expenditures.

The *Family Guy* parody of *Schoolhouse Rock's* "I'm Just a Bill" song closely resembles the fate of most bills; a Capitol custodian promptly throws the singing bill into the trash.

Criticisms of Congress

If you look back over the last 50 years, you will find only a handful of instances when more than 50% of Americans approved of Congress. Why all the criticism? There are three main reasons, listed in increasing order of how much they drive citizens crazy.

 Logrolling: When members of Congress exchange favors and/or votes, constituents feel betrayed.

 Pork Barrel Spending: When elected officials put their own districts or states before the country as a whole, wasteful spending ends up being added—usually in the form of amendments—to a bill. This not only slows down the approval process, but also sometimes causes an important bill to fail.

 Inefficiency: When the members of Congress cannot compromise, the federal government shuts down. As of the 1980s, an increasingly partisan rift between Republicans and Democrats has caused this to happen on 12 occasions.

If you've finished reading this section and think that Congress is just like high school...you're 100% correct.

The President and the Executive Branch ❗

The president is both the head of state and head of government. The president arguably wields more political power than any other American. However, to be an effective leader, the president must work with Congress and the courts.

So You Want to Be President? ❗

Despite the importance of the presidency, there are surprisingly few requirements for the job.

Following the passage of the Twenty-Second Amendment (1951), no one can be elected president more than twice. However, if the vice president has to succeed the president (due to illness, death, impeachment, or resignation) and serves fewer than two years before re-election, the vice president (now president) can still campaign for two more full terms.

Regardless of where you were born, if your mother was an American citizen, you fit this category.

These 14 years do not have to be consecutive.

APPLICATION
for the Presidency of the United States

Job Title: President of the United States
Duration: 4–10 years
Location: Washington, D.C.
(Furnished Home Provided)
Salary: $400,000/Year
Benefits: Generous Pension, Medical Insurance, and Secret Service Protection for Life

Questionnaire:
1. Are you 35+ years old? **Y/N**
2. Are you a natural-born citizen? **Y/N**
3. Have you lived in the United States for 14+ years? **Y/N**

If you answered yes to each question, you may proceed with the next step of the application process: petitioning each of the 50 states for a spot on November's ballot.

Formal Powers of the President ❶

The president's schedule is always full, but Article 2 Section II of the Constitution grants the president only a handful of formal powers and responsibilities.

Presidential To-Do List

☐ Act as Commander in Chief of the Armed Forces—This is this is the broadest of the powers entrusted to the president, as they are unspecified.

☐ Grant Pardons or Reprieves—The president has the power to forgive individuals of crimes or have their sentences commuted, or ended early.

☐ Convene Congress at Any Time

☐ Make Treaties with Other Nations (Need 2/3 Senate Approval)

☐ Appoint Ambassadors and Federal Court Judges (Need 2/3 Senate Approval)

☐ Execute Congress's Laws—This portion of the Constitution lays the foundation for the structure of bureaucracies with the president at the lead.

☐ Receive Ambassadors from Other Nations

☐ Sign (or Veto) Congress's Legislation—A **pocket veto** is the term given to running out the clock on Congress. If fewer than 10 days remain in the session and the president refuses to sign a bill, that bill has to start over again from scratch at the start of the next session. Many U.S. governors employ the **line-item veto,** but with a brief exception in the1990s, the president is not permitted to veto only specific parts of a bill. The Supreme Court deemed it an unconstitutional violation of the balance of power between the legislative and executive branches.

☐ Update Congress (and the Public) about the State of the Union

"Advice and Consent" ❗

When it comes to appointing judges or making treaties with other nations—that is, dealing with the laws of this country and those of others—the president is checked and balanced by the Constitution's "advice and consent" line, which stipulates that this part of the president's power must come with the Senate's approval.

Senatorial courtesy occurs when a federal judge seat opens up in a state and the president follows the suggestions of that state's two senators in appointing a replacement.

 Ask Yourself...

Why might the president extend senatorial courtesy to a senator not in the president's party?

The President's Unofficial Duties and Support System 💬

From congratulating winning sports teams to comforting Americans in a time of crisis, the president has many unofficial duties not mentioned in the Constitution. The first lady and White House staff help the president with his unofficial duties.

Unofficial Role	Example
Agenda Setter	From his position of power, the president can influence the actions of Congress and the courts. If the president's party controls Congress, the president can set Congress's legislative agenda. Also, by simply speaking to the press, the president can advertise his agenda to the entire nation.
Morale Builder	As the public face of the United States, people look to the president in a time of crisis. Three days after the terrorist attacks of September 11, 2001, President George W. Bush visited Ground Zero in New York City to personally thank rescue workers for searching for survivors.

Support System	Role/Example
The First Lady	The president may be the public face of the United States, but the first lady is the public face of the White House. Throughout U.S. history, first ladies have taken a greater role by applying their recognition to important projects. For example, First Lady Michelle Obama fought to improve the nutrition of public school lunches.
The White House Staff	The White House staff assist the president with his formal and informal duties. From speechwriting to scheduling, they help the president advance his agenda. All members of the White House staff report to the president's chief of staff.

 Ask Yourself...

Research the president's actions over the last week. What official and unofficial duties has the president performed?

Expanded Powers ❗

Presidential power has expanded tremendously since the nation's founding. One way to track the growth of presidential power is through the increase of executive orders issued by presidents. These orders direct the actions of the federal government, carry the weight of law, but are subject to judicial review. In the graph, the number of executive orders signed by each president appears above the president's name.

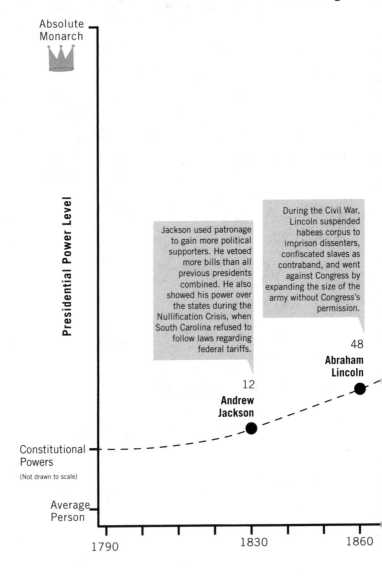

Absolute
Monarch

Presidential Power Level

Jackson used patronage to gain more political supporters. He vetoed more bills than all previous presidents combined. He also showed his power over the states during the Nullification Crisis, when South Carolina refused to follow laws regarding federal tariffs.

During the Civil War, Lincoln suspended habeas corpus to imprison dissenters, confiscated slaves as contraband, and went against Congress by expanding the size of the army without Congress's permission.

48
**Abraham
Lincoln**

12
**Andrew
Jackson**

Constitutional
Powers

(Not drawn to scale)

Average
Person

1790   1830   1860

Presidential Power

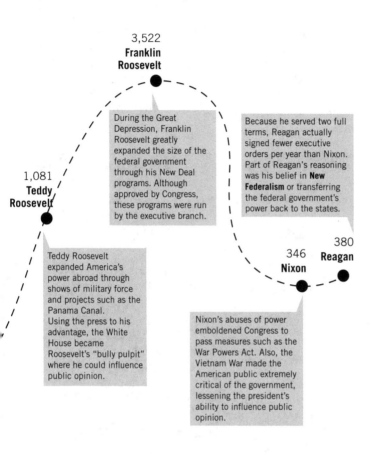

3,522
**Franklin
Roosevelt**

During the Great
Depression, Franklin
Roosevelt greatly
expanded the size of the
federal government
through his New Deal
programs. Although
approved by Congress,
these programs were run
by the executive branch.

Because he served two full
terms, Reagan actually
signed fewer executive
orders per year than Nixon.
Part of Reagan's reasoning
was his belief in **New
Federalism** or transferring
the federal government's
power back to the states.

1,081
**Teddy
Roosevelt**

380
Reagan

346
Nixon

Teddy Roosevelt
expanded America's
power abroad through
shows of military force
and projects such as the
Panama Canal.
Using the press to his
advantage, the White
House became
Roosevelt's "bully pulpit"
where he could influence
public opinion.

Nixon's abuses of power
emboldened Congress to
pass measures such as the
War Powers Act. Also, the
Vietnam War made the
American public extremely
critical of the government,
lessening the president's
ability to influence public
opinion.

1900   1930   1970   1981

History

 To give you an idea of how constantly surrounded the president is by people and duties (both official and unofficial), President Herbert Hoover (1929–33) actually spoke in Mandarin Chinese to his wife, Lou, so as to have some privacy.

Commander in Chief in the Nuclear Age ❶

The invention of nuclear weapons radically changed the president's role as commander in chief. In an emergency situation, the president, not Congress, would need to make a quick decision about whether to obliterate another country. Congress has tackled this new reality by passing resolutions that have expanded (and contracted) the president's power to wage war. Here are a few of the biggest changes.

Year	Law	Effect
1964	Gulf of Tonkin Resolution	Congress granted President Johnson broad powers to pursue a war in Vietnam. Johnson committed 500,000+ soldiers to the war effort without a declaration of war.
1973	War Powers Act	The War Powers Act was passed as a result of President Nixon expanding the Vietnam War in Cambodia and Laos. Presidents now need Congress's permission to continue a military conflict after 30 days of fighting. If not, Congress can stop funding military action. Congress has never used the War Powers Act to stop a military conflict.
2002	Iraq Resolution	Congress gave President George W. Bush the authority to use military force to depose Iraq's dictator, Saddam Hussein. In March 2003, 190,000 American soldiers invaded Iraq.

One of the reasons that Congress has not declared war since 1941 is that during the Cold War (1945–89), lawmakers feared that declaring war would heighten tensions (and possibly lead to a nuclear war) between the United States and Soviet Union.

In what ways has presidential power increased (or decreased) in the last ten years?

The Vice President

Besides becoming president if the current president should die, resign, or become incapacitated, the vice president's only two responsibilities are **casting a tie-breaking vote in the Senate** and **officiating the results of the Electoral College**. It's not a very long job description, and the position is light on actual power.

Even so, presidential candidates have to put a lot of thought into who should be their vice presidential candidates. Before 1804, though, the process was a lot simpler.

Before 1804, the runner-up in the presidential election became vice president.

The 12th Amendment (1804) changed the selection process of the vice president. Presidential candidates could now select their own running mates. Now when a presidential candidate is looking for a vice presidential candidate, he or she has a checklist in mind, one that reveals a modern vice president's role in the executive branch.

 "I have not seen *The Hunger Games*. Not enough class warfare for me."

—President Barack Obama at the White House Correspondents' Dinner

APPLICATION
for the Vice Presidency of the United States

Dear Potential Vice Presidents,

Please answer the following questions truthfully. Any negative replies will likely disqualify you from becoming my vice president.

Sincerely Yours,

The (Hopefully) Future President

- Crucial: Do you meet all the requirements for president? **Y / N**
- Do you have government experience?   **Y / N**
- Do you come from a swing state? **Y / N**
- Are you liked there? **Y / N**
- Are you free of any baggage/scandals? **Y / N**
- If I ask you for your opinion, will you give it to me straight? **Y / N**
- When my term(s) are up, would you be interested in running for president? **Y / N**

Ask Yourself...

What are other reasons that the current vice president was chosen by the current president?

The 25th Amendment ❗

In 1841, 1865, 1901, and 1963, active U.S. presidents died as a result of natural causes or assassination, and the vice president served out the remainder of the term. As of 1967, the 25th Amendment has made this succession procedure more explicit:

- In the case of the president's death or resignation, the vice president is the official successor.

- In the case of the vice president's death or resignation, the president must replace the vice president.
- In the case of the president becoming ill or otherwise incapacitated, the vice president can be temporarily declared the acting president. (This can be done either by the president **or** by the cabinet and Congress.)

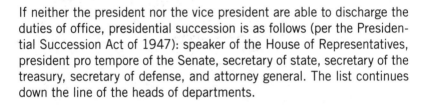

In 2002 and 2007, President George W. Bush invoked the 25th Amendment to temporarily appoint Vice President Dick Cheney as Acting President. Why? On both occasions, President Bush was undergoing a colonoscopy. *

The Line of Succession ∽

If neither the president nor the vice president are able to discharge the duties of office, presidential succession is as follows (per the Presidential Succession Act of 1947): speaker of the House of Representatives, president pro tempore of the Senate, secretary of state, secretary of the treasury, secretary of defense, and attorney general. The list continues down the line of the heads of departments.

The Cabinet ❶

As the nation grew in size and complexity, lawmakers realized that the president needed help managing the new duties of the executive branch. Starting in 1789, Congress began creating executive departments to assist the president. The president controlled these departments, but only the Senate could approve the department's leader, known as the secretary. These secretaries make up the president's cabinet. Today, the cabinet consists of 15 secretaries and their departments.

A cabinet secretary is his or her executive department's greatest advocate. If his or her department should make a mistake, it is the cabinet secretary, and not the president, who takes the fall.

---

 * Don't know what a colonoscopy is? You will.

In the "cabinet" below, the larger the jar, the larger the executive department.

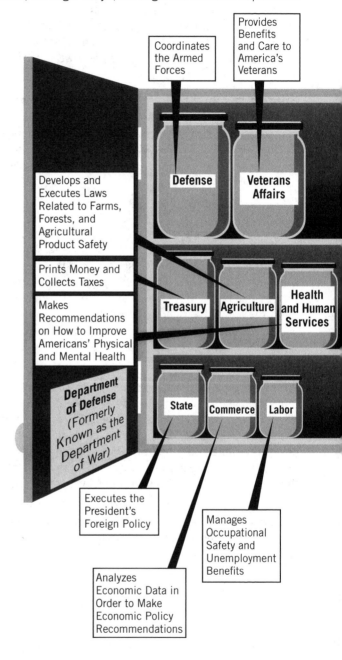

Coordinates the Armed Forces

Provides Benefits and Care to America's Veterans

Develops and Executes Laws Related to Farms, Forests, and Agricultural Product Safety

Prints Money and Collects Taxes

Makes Recommendations on How to Improve Americans' Physical and Mental Health

Department of Defense (Formerly Known as the Department of War)

Defense

Veterans Affairs

Treasury **Agriculture** **Health and Human Services**

State **Commerce** **Labor**

Executes the President's Foreign Policy

Manages Occupational Safety and Unemployment Benefits

Analyzes Economic Data in Order to Make Economic Policy Recommendations

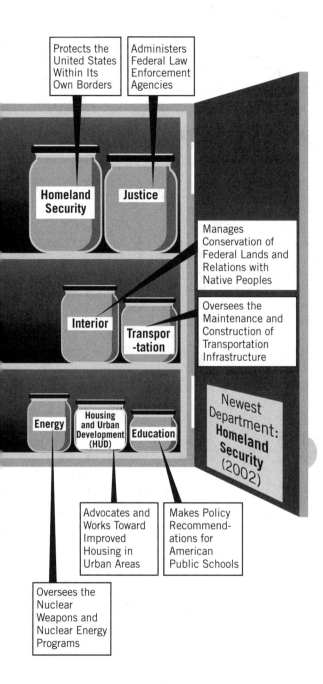

Protects the United States Within Its Own Borders

Administers Federal Law Enforcement Agencies

Homeland Security

Justice

Manages Conservation of Federal Lands and Relations with Native Peoples

Oversees the Maintenance and Construction of Transportation Infrastructure

Interior

Transpor-tation

Newest Department: Homeland Security (2002)

Energy

Housing and Urban Development (HUD)

Education

Advocates and Works Toward Improved Housing in Urban Areas

Makes Policy Recommend-ations for American Public Schools

Oversees the Nuclear Weapons and Nuclear Energy Programs

The Executive Departments ❗

Related to the executive departments are dozens of government agencies. Some of these agencies are directly administered by an executive department, while others are independent. Even independent agencies still answer directly to the executive branch.

Directly Administered	Independent
• Office of Management and Budget (OMB): Creates the president's national budget. *Reports directly to the president.* • Federal Bureau of Investigation (FBI): Gathers intelligence within the United States. *Reports to the Department of Justice.* • Census Bureau: Administers the national census every 10 years. *Reports to the Department of Commerce.* • Drug Enforcement Administration (DEA): Combats drug traffic and drug use within the United States. *Reports to the Department of Justice.*	• Central Intelligence Agency (CIA): Gathers intelligence on foreign individuals and foreign governments. • Federal Reserve Board: Creates the monetary policy for the United States. • Federal Trade Commission (FTC): Protects consumers from monopolies. • National Aeronautics and Space Administration (NASA): Administers the space program and develops new space technologies. • National Labor Relations Board (NLRB): Investigates and solves unfair labor practices. • Securities and Exchange Commission (SEC): Enforces federal law regarding financial investing.

Ask Yourself...

Has the creation of executive departments expanded the president's power, or decentralized the executive branch of government?

The White House Offices ❗

Since 1939, the president has relied upon trusted peers for advice on the innumerable issues that the country may face. The president chooses the members of each office, and does not require Senate approval. As of the writing of this book, there are 20 White House offices that help to craft the nation's foreign and domestic policies. Below is a chart that highlights the hierarchy of these offices along with an explanation of what some of them do.

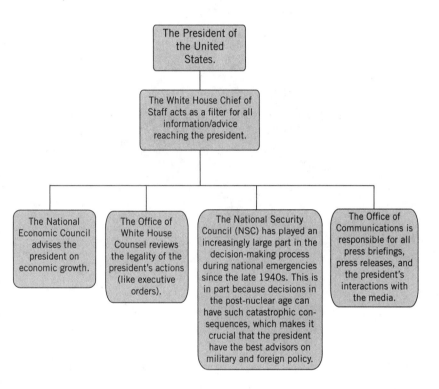

The Bureaucracy 🛑

The bureaucracy comprises all *other* employees of the federal government. In this bureaucracy, 2.7 million employees are civilians, and the total number of employees rises to 4.1 million when including U.S. military personnel. Though Congress authorizes all funding for these employees, the bureaucracy itself is under the control of the executive branch.

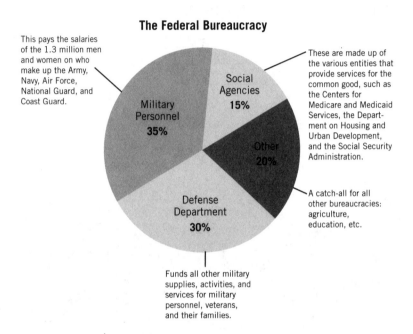

The Federal Bureaucracy

This pays the salaries of the 1.3 million men and women on who make up the Army, Navy, Air Force, National Guard, and Coast Guard.

These are made up of the various entities that provide services for the common good, such as the Centers for Medicare and Medicaid Services, the Department on Housing and Urban Development, and the Social Security Administration.

Military Personnel 35%

Social Agencies 15%

Other 20%

Defense Department 30%

A catch-all for all other bureaucracies: agriculture, education, etc.

Funds all other military supplies, activities, and services for military personnel, veterans, and their families.

Qualifications 💬

Since the passage of the Pendleton Act (1883), all applicants to the federal bureaucracy must score highly on one of many different civil service exams. The Pendleton Act also ended the **spoils system,** through which presidents would reward supporters with government jobs. Today, the Office of Personnel Management (OPM) uses this test-based merit system to select the most qualified candidates.

The Bureaucracy Expands 💬

During the Great Depression, President Roosevelt greatly expanded the federal bureaucracy by creating 100+ federal agencies. Due to the use of acronyms, these agencies became known as Roosevelt's "alphabet agencies." Many of these agencies still exist today.

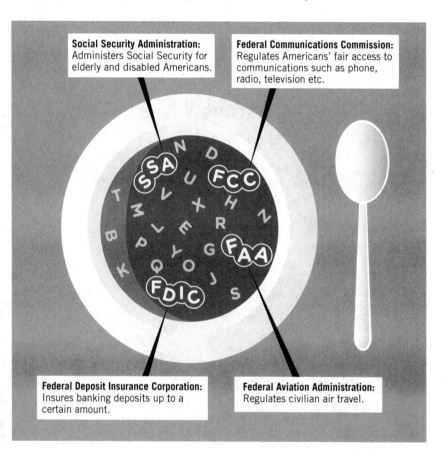

Social Security Administration: Administers Social Security for elderly and disabled Americans.

Federal Communications Commission: Regulates Americans' fair access to communications such as phone, radio, television etc.

Federal Deposit Insurance Corporation: Insures banking deposits up to a certain amount.

Federal Aviation Administration: Regulates civilian air travel.

Government Deregulation 🌀

Following the extreme growth of the bureaucracy during the Great Depression, Congress has since dissolved some of the smaller executive regulatory agencies. These changes are often the result of lobbyists who want more freedom in their industry and because of legislators who favor shrinking the size (and budget) of the federal government. The Civil Aeronautics Board and Interstate Commerce Commission, which regulated air and ground travel, respectively, were abolished in the 1960s and 1990s.

Government Corporations: Where the Public and Private Sectors Meet 🌀

If you've ever listened to public radio, chances are you've tuned in during a pledge drive. The cheery announcer tells you, "We'd really love to get back to [What you want to listen to], but we need your support." Just about every public-private partnership works this way. The following organizations are run like corporations, but receive different levels of government funding.

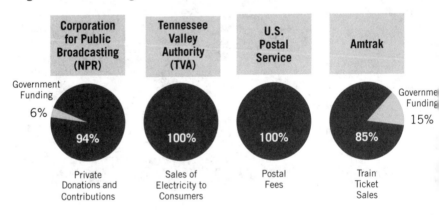

The Judiciary 😮

With the Supreme Court at its apex, the federal judiciary interprets federal law. Each federal judge is handpicked by the president, but all must pass confirmation by the Senate. When a federal judge hears a case, he or she always considers whether or not someone's constitutional rights were violated.

The Supreme Court 😮

Article III of the U.S. Constitution established the Supreme Court and gave Congress the power to create "inferior" courts to hear disputes of federal law. To ensure an independent judiciary, the Constitution forbids the lowering of a federal judge's salary. However, it is possible for Congress to impeach federal court judges and justices on the Supreme Court. The latter has never happened.

Appointing the Justices 😮

The Senate decides whether to confirm the selection of a Supreme Court justice through confirmation hearings. Here, they ask "litmus test" questions that get a sense for where a justice will potentially stand on hot-button social issues such as abortion and gun control. However, because nominees need the support of the Senate, they often provide vague answers.

> " I have offered no promises on how I'd rule to anyone on any case."
>
> —Neil Gorsuch, 2017

The Chief Justice

Though each justice on the Supreme Court has an equal vote, the Chief Justice (appointed by the president) has extra responsibilities:

1. represents the Court in public appearances
2. leads the proceedings when the Court is in session
3. chooses who (of those who voted for it) writes the majority opinion*

* This happens only if the chief justice sides with the majority. If not, the most senior justice who supports that opinion makes this decision.

Have There Always Been Nine Justices?

Nothing in the Constitution requires the Supreme Court to have nine (or any number) of justices. From its creation in 1789 until passage of the Judiciary Act of 1869, the court fluctuated from as few as 5 to as many as 10 members before settling at the 9 we have today. In the 1930s, President Roosevelt attempted to expand the Court's size to 15. Roosevelt's critics accused him of "court packing," and Roosevelt eventually gave up on his plan.

 Ask Yourself...

How does a president's choice of Supreme Court justice affect that president's legacy?

Judicial Review ❗

Early in its history, the Supreme Court's power expanded under the leadership of John Marshall, who served as chief justice between 1801 and 1835. A federalist who believed in the federal government's power over that of the states, Chief Justice Marshall oversaw cases that redefined the Court's role as a branch of government.

Year	Case	Result
1803	*Marbury v. Madison*	The Court redefined its ability to declare federal laws constitutional or not, in an act now known as **judicial review**.
1810	*Fletcher v. Peck*	The Court extended its right of judicial review to laws passed by the states.

How a Case Reaches the Supreme Court ❗

In general, a case works its way through the federal court system, with the Supreme Court not granting an appeal until all opportunities have been exhausted in the lower appellate courts. This is done in part to ensure that the cases are real and adverse, with an actual legal dispute at their core, and not just a political issue. Nothing is hypothetical, and there must be a petitioner to bring the initial case, one who has a vested interest in the outcome (this is called **standing**). However, if the Court feels strongly about reviewing a lower court's decision, they can take up the case regardless of where it is in the system. This more immediate response occurs when the Court grants a **writ of *certiorari***.

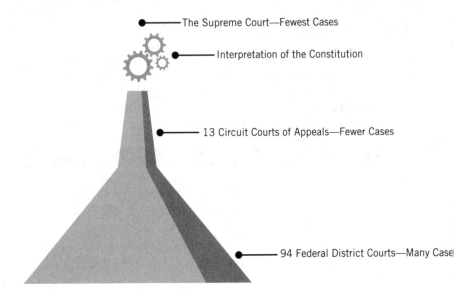

- The Supreme Court—Fewest Cases
- Interpretation of the Constitution
- 13 Circuit Courts of Appeals—Fewer Cases
- 94 Federal District Courts—Many Cases

Federal Judiciary Air Filter

1. A case comes before a Federal District Court. This court has original jurisdiction over a case. This is a trial court, and juries decide guilt or innocence in civil and criminal cases.

2. If the ruling is appealed, the case goes before a Circuit Courts of Appeals. As the Supreme Court does, judges decide solely whether a constitutional right was violated and do not review the facts of a case. It is at this point that the Supreme Court usually issues a writ of certiorari to bring a case up to the Court. It is very unlikely that the Supreme Court will do so after the Circuit Court has ruled on a case.

3. Lawyers for both sides submit briefs to the Court. These documents explain the case from the petitioner and respondent's point of view.

4. Before the case is heard, interest groups looking to sway the Court's decision may submit *amicus curiae* ("friend of the court") briefs.

5. The justices hear cases.

6. The justices, with the help of their clerks, research precedents set by previous Court decisions, which may help to guide their decisions. When the Court agrees with previous rulings, it is known as *stare decisis.*

7. The justices vote.

8. Once voting is complete, the majority and minority opinions are assigned to and written up by specific justices. Any other justice is free to write a concurring or a dissenting opinion.

9. The Court announces its decisions in May, June, and July.

Arguing a Case at the Supreme Court 💬

*From October to April, the Supreme Court hears its annual docket of cases. During a case, lawyers from both sides have 30 minutes each to present their arguments. At any time, a justice may interrupt a lawyer to ask questions or make statements about what they have just heard. If the petitioner or respondent in a case is the U.S. Government, the U.S. solicitor general acts as the government's attorney.

Judicial Activism vs. Judicial Restraint ❗

Judicial restraint is exercised by a justice who is hesitant to overturn federal law, and interprets the Constitution literally. For example, Justice Antonin Scalia considered himself to be a strict constructionist, someone who believes that justices should not interpret the Constitution based on personal belief or society's changing attitudes on issues.

Judicial activism is exercised by a justice who is more likely to overturn federal law and to work from personal belief when making a decision. For example, Justice Thurgood Marshall believed that the Constitution was a "living document," something that a justice was not meant to simply follow.

United States v. Forty-Three Gallons of Whisky (1863) was an actual Supreme Court case. Unfortunately, *Deflated Footballs v. The New England Patriots* (2016) was not.

The Changing Court 💬

As various civil rights movements transformed America in the 19th and 20th centuries, the Supreme Court saw its makeup become more diverse:

1916	Louis Brandeis becomes the first Jewish Supreme Court Justice.
1967	Thurgood Marshall becomes the first black Supreme Court Justice.
1981	Sandra Day O'Connor becomes the first female Supreme Court Justice.
1986	Antonin Scalia becomes the first Italian-American Supreme Court Justice.
2009	Sonia Sotomayor becomes the first Hispanic-American Supreme Court Justice.

As of 2017, all members of the Supreme Court were raised Jewish or Roman Catholic. This is a 180° change from the Court's first 180 years, when all the justices were Protestant.

Ask Yourself...

Does the Supreme Court's greater diversity have an effect on its decisions? Should it?

Federal and State Judiciaries Compared ⌇

Just as the federal government is responsible for setting up the federal court system to try cases regarding federal law, states have a similar system to try cases regarding state law. A state's supreme court is that state's highest legal authority.

It is rare that a case would transfer from a state court to a federal court, but there is **one big exception**: when one side of a case believes that a state law violates the Constitution.

Relationships, Balance of Power ❗

To make sure that no branch of government becomes too powerful, the Constitution mandates an official balance of power that puts each branch in competition with the other two. Additionally, there is an unofficial balance of power that keeps the government running: Representatives must fulfill the needs of constituents and interest groups while working within the parameters of bureaucratic regulations.

The Official Balance of Power ❗

Before reviewing the unofficial balance of power that exists within the federal government, take a moment to review the constitutional checks and balances that exist among the three branches.

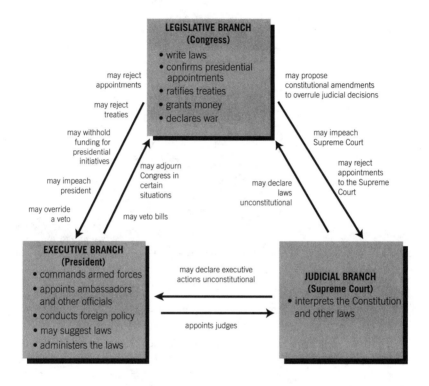

The Unofficial Balance of Power ❗

At the heart of the unofficial balance of power are "iron triangles" that define the relationships among Congress, interest groups, and the bureaucracy.

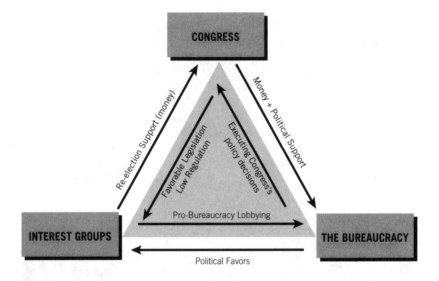

In an iron triangle, an interest group lobbies the members of a congressional committee (e.g., promising campaign funds) to affect the workings of a bureaucratic agency, usually a regulatory agency that affects a company that pays for the interest group.

Though the bureaucratic leadership serves at the pleasure of the president, most of its employees are career officials. In many cases, career advancement depends on forming productive relationships with Congress and interest groups.

 If you haven't guessed already, iron triangles work on the concept of *quid pro quo*, or 'You scratch my back, I'll scratch yours.'

Criticisms of the Bureaucracy and Iron Triangles ❗

Inefficiency

The government takes too long to provide essential services; this is known as "red tape."

Example: Former soldiers struggle to receive timely medical treatment through the Department of Veterans Affairs. Some veterans remain on waiting lists for months if not years.

Redundancy

Two departments do the same job, which wastes money.

Example: Both the FBI and Department of Homeland Security investigate domestic threats.

Incoordination

As the number of government agencies increases, the communication between them drops.

Example: In the lead-up to the terrorist attacks on September 11, 2001, the inability of law enforcement and intelligence agencies to efficiently share information with one another played a role in allowing terrorists to enter the United States.

Fraud

Iron triangles can lead to immoral/illegal actions.

Example: If a lobbying group is able to convince Congress to lower environmental regulations, certain companies may release toxic chemicals in the water, ground, and air.

Redundancy

Two departments do the same job, which wastes money.

Example: Both the FBI and Department of Homeland Security investigate domestic threats.

Unaccountability

Bureaucrats do not answer directly to the American people.

Example: The complexity of a bureaucracy makes it easy to pass along the blame for a mistake, which makes it difficult to remove those who were responsible.

 Did you notice that the entry for Redundancy appeared twice? That's a feature, not a bug.

Linkages 🛈

Besides constitutional relationships and iron triangles, the branches of government are linked together by other forces. Voters, interest groups, political parties, media, and local governments affect the workings of the federal government.

Interest Groups 🛈

In addition to their role in iron triangles, interest groups publicly promote the beliefs of a particular political party or politician running for office. In an election season, interest groups' activities include buying television advertising and sending mailers to voters. These activities have the potential to swing elections.

Interest groups can be classified into one of three categories: liberal, conservative, or middle of the road. The last group often splits its money between both political parties.

Liberal	Middle of the Road	Conservative
• MoveOn.org supports liberal Democratic candidates in local and national elections.	• The American Medical Association (AMA) gives most of its donations to support Republican candidates, but it has supported Democratic causes such as President Obama's Affordable Care Act.	• The U.S. Chamber of Commerce spends more money than any other interest group. It promotes the expansion of American businesses.
• The AFL-CIO represents over 12 million union members in the United States. It overwhelmingly supports Democratic candidates.	• The mission of the American Israel Public Affairs Committee (AIPAC) is to promote continued U.S. support for the State of Israel. It regularly donates money to both Republican and Democratic candidates.	• The National Rifle Organization (NRA) has fought for more than 140 years against legislation that would restrict gun ownership in the United States.

Public Opinion and Voters ❗

Every election cycle, politicians spend hundreds of millions of dollars to gauge voters' opinions on innumerable issues. From phone calls to focus groups, candidates want to know what's inside voters' minds. And once the results are in, the vast majority of politicians will adjust their positions in order to win an election.

> "However [political parties] may now and then answer popular ends, they are likely in the course of time and things, to become potent engines, by which cunning, ambitious, and unprincipled men will be enabled to subvert the power of the people and to usurp for themselves the reins of government, destroying afterwards the very engines which have lifted them to unjust dominion."

—George Washington, *Farewell Address*

Political Parties and Ideology ❗

Political parties are driven by ideology, and over time a party's ideology can change. For example, though the Democratic and Republican parties have existed since the 19th century, their ideologies have flipped over the last 75 years. That's why it is best to think in terms of the underlying ideology and not the name of the political party.

 On the television show *House of Cards*, the corrupt President Frank Underwood offers the following piece of advice: "When the money is coming your way, don't ask any questions."

Ideology	Beliefs
Conservative	• Individuals responsible for themselves • Limited government involvement in people's lives • Free, unregulated markets
Liberal	• Government involvement to fix social/economic injustices • Opposition to laws/initiatives based on religion
Moderate (a.k.a. Independent)	• No adherence to a specific ideology • Hold some conservative and liberal beliefs

The Problems with Ideology ❗

People with firm ideologies come into conflict with one another. This is likelier to happen during economic recessions, when more Americans abandon moderate viewpoints, and align themselves with conservative or liberal ideology. Throughout U.S. history, political partisanship has led to the following:

- The Polarization of Citizens' Political Beliefs
- Distrust of Other Americans
- Government Inefficiencies
- Government Shutdowns
- The Civil War

Isn't the Supreme Court Independent of Politics? 💬

In theory, yes. Yet with the Senate confirming potential justices along strict party lines, it is easy to predict how the changing Court will support the president and Congress's legislative agenda.

Ask Yourself...

Read the news from the last seven days. What problems has partisanship caused?

The Media 🔔

Although the media isn't part of the federal government, their influence has led some to refer to them as the fourth estate, an unofficial check on government power. By appealing to the public, the media can quickly shift public opinion.

Watchdog	The media, like many government regulatory agencies, acts as a watchdog on government action. Exposing abuses of power or mismanagement can quickly cause the government to change its actions.
Advocate	Through editorials, powerful media outlets can lend support to (or protest against) politicians, government programs, and bills.
Spotlight	The media often give a voice to smaller political organizations/causes. Grassroots organizations often rely on media coverage to raise their support among Americans.

State Governments 🔔

Compared to the federal government, state governments are considerably smaller in terms of employees and annual spending. Yet some states, like California, have such large populations and concentrations of industry that they greatly influence not only their neighbors, but also the federal government.

"As California goes, so goes the nation."

California has been a leader in a number of different ways:

California was the first state to pass anti-stalking laws, which were quickly adopted by other states.

The anti-pollution laws passed by California have been taken up by more than ten other states.

California's strict fuel efficiency standards have been adopted by other states.

California was the first state to cut property tax increases in the 1970s.

California led the fight for nationwide gay marriage.

CHAPTER 5

Public Policy

Public policy attempts to solve (or prevent) America's domestic problems through legislation and the actions of regulatory agencies. However, making effective public policy is more than just law. Everyone, from the president to ordinary Americans, is involved in the public policy process.

Federal Policy Making ❗

Enacting policies is critical, as it is the mechanism through which the government delivers services to the citizenry. However, policy making often requires competing individuals and interests to compromise to arrive at an agreeable solution. Follow the cards below to see how public policy gets shuffled out.

Round 1: RECOGNIZING

Explanation: Policy making begins with identifying an issue that needs to be addressed.

Social Problems

High crime rates, high unemployment, poverty, and addiction

Threats

Terrorism and war

Objectives

Building a highway, exploring outer space, and curing disease, to name just a few

Public Opinion

Desires and grievances from individuals, interest groups, and industry all sway the public agenda.

Issue-Attention Cycle

Issues make it to the top of the deck when they hold public attention. Lawmakers are quick to act on issues that dominate headlines, cable news, and social media feeds

Round 2: PLANNING

Explanation: Policy making often involves conflict, debate, and compromise.

Special Interest Groups

United around changing a specific policy

Lobbyists

Attempt to sway policy for their special interest group.

Incrementalism

A slow, step-by-step approach to making policy that aims to avoid unforeseen results and to moderate bitter disputes

Round 3: FORMALIZING

Explanation: There are a number of ways to enact policy.

Legislative Process

Passing a bill through the Congress

Executive Orders

A direct policy from the president

Supreme Court Decision

The setting or reversing of precedent so as to change the law

Regulatory Agency Ruling

Agencies can enact policy for their specific departments, like the EPA.

Round 4: IMPLEMENTING

Explanation: The way in which policies are rolled out.

Timetables

Schedules clarify the dates by which new policies are to be enforced.

Enforcement

Grants and tax breaks incentivize states and individuals to adhere to the new policy. Punishments like fines or prison sentences ensure that people obey the rules.

Fragmentation

Too much focus on individual portions of a larger problem—like the War on Drugs—can lead to conflicting policies from the Army, Navy, Air Force, Coast Guard, Border Patrol, etc.

Round 5: EVALUATING

Explanation: Does a policy actually work in the real world?

Feedback

Data and opinions are collected to see how the policy works.

Modification

Tweaks are proposed and adapted.

Success

You win! (We'd say "everybody wins," but not every policy helps everybody.)

Unintended Consequences

Some policies fulfill one purpose while also causing more severe issues; for instance, the "three-strike rule" was meant to get career criminals off the street but instead caused more trials and overloaded courts.

Clean Up (Reshuffling)

If the evaluation of a policy creates no problems, congratulations: You've won! If, however, the policy has failed or led to unforeseen consequences, you'll have to reshuffle and start over again in the planning phase; that's right, the final evaluation may double as recognizing a problem, one that the government itself has created.

Government Economics

Fiscal policy, the means by which the government raises and spends money, lays the foundation for all other government action. In the United States, the budget is proposed by the White House, but managed by a variety of committees in Congress.

> The **Director of the Office of Management and Budget (OMB)** works off the president's policy initiatives to initiate the budget process. This is based on the health of the economy, specifically government revenue projections, which is the predicted income from taxes. Based on the priorities of the executive branch, some departments will receive more money than others.
>
> After Congress receives the proposed budget, the leadership sends it to three committees.

The **House Ways and Means Committee** deals with the taxing aspects of the budget.	**Authorization committees** in both houses decide what programs Congress wants to fund.	**Appropriations committees** in both houses then decide how much money to spend for those programs that have been authorized.

 Ask Yourself...

Research a public policy that affects your home state. Try to identify the cards from "Federal Policy Making" that apply to it. Is the policy being held up due to fiscal constraints?

Legislative Disagreements

The budget process is complicated, politically divisive, and in recent years, nearly impossible to conclude. That's because the president and the two political parties in Congress often fight over the projected revenues and proposed expenditures.

Budget Reform Act of 1974

 This act created the **Congressional Budget Office**, which allows committees in both the House and Senate to limit their own revenue and spending levels.

 Negotiations take place between the White House and the two houses of Congress in an effort to create one budget acceptable to everyone. Failure to achieve a budget by the beginning of the **fiscal year** could mean shutting down the government and sending employees home.

 In a shutdown, budget stopgap bills temporarily appropriate money to keep the most critical portions of government operating.

The Budget Enforcement Act of 1990

 This act attempted to streamline the reforms from 1974 so as to more easily compromise on budgets.

 Government expenditures are categorized as either mandatory or discretionary.

 Mandatory spending, required by law, funds the following entitlement programs: Social Security, Medicare, Medicaid, veterans' pensions, and repayment of the national debt.

 Discretionary spending, which is not required by law, includes defense, education, highways, research grants, all government operations, and any healthcare spending not covered by Medicare and Medicaid.

 Discretionary programs are the primary targets for making cuts to balance the budget.

Fiscal Revenue 🔔

Before the federal government spends money, it gathers revenue and creates budgets.

Revenues, by Major Source

Percentage of Gross Domestic Product

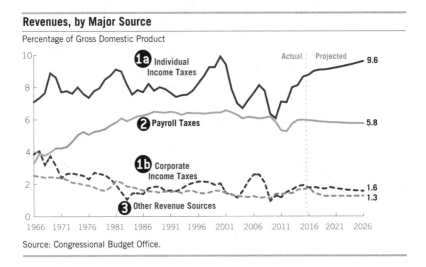

Source: Congressional Budget Office.

1a **Individual Income Taxes** A progressive tax increases tax rates for people with higher incomes. Those citizens at the poverty level, for example, may pay few or no taxes. Middle-class citizens may be taxed at a 15% rate, while the wealthy are taxed at two or three times that rate. The goal of a progressive tax is to allow those with greater need to keep more of what they earn while taking more from those who can best afford it. The Internal Revenue Service is tasked with the responsibility of collecting all individual income taxes.

1b **Corporate Income Taxes** Like individuals, resident corporations in the United States pay income taxes to the federal government.

2 **Social Insurance (Payroll) Taxes** These specific taxes go toward maintaining specific programs, like Social Security, Unemployment benefits, and other national insurance programs.

3 **Other Revenue Sources** Money is also collected through a variety of other fines and fees. A **sales tax** is handled at the state level, but the federal government may also levy an additional flat **excise tax** against products such as fuel, alcohol, tobacco, and airfare.

Mandatory Spending and Entitlements

Before the **Great Depression**, there were no government programs to help people who suffered from hardships. But during the 1930s, so many people needed help that the government enacted programs to create jobs, provide housing, and feed the hungry. Social safety net programs such as these were expanded under the Johnson administration and are now sometimes called **entitlements.** As the government is compelled to provide entitlements by law, they make up a large portion of the nation's mandatory spending.

Social insurance programs are in reality national insurance programs into which employers and employees pay taxes. Because individuals pay into these programs, the benefits derived are considered by the public to have been earned.

Social Security is an entitlement program mandated by law and into which all working citizens pay a percentage of their earnings. Since 1935, the government has paid benefits to all people who meet the requirements of the program (retired and disabled people). Changing the law would require congressional action. Because the largest voting block of the electorate is made up of those nearing or at retirement age, there is little chance of major changes to the system. However, some experts warn that the Social Security trust fund will go bankrupt in the near future.

Medicare provides government assistance to people older than 65 for health care. The high and rising cost of health care has led some to question the solvency of this program, but recent reports note that it is more than able to cover 100% of its costs through at least 2030.	**Medicaid** provides medical and health-related services for low-income parents, children, seniors, and people with disabilities. It is jointly funded by the states and federal government and is managed and run by the individual states.	**Unemployment Insurance** provides a weekly benefit to those who are out of work (for a limited time). Each state government administers its own unemployment insurance program. Both the federal and state governments pay into a trust fund to provide the benefit.

Public assistance programs are not perceived as earned. Recipients are not required to pay into the system to get something out. Public assistance is considered by some to be a "handout" to the undeserving. Because of this public perception, public policy initiatives from both parties often force people on public assistance to seek work or enter work-training programs.

Welfare Programs, also known as Aid to Families with Dependent Children (AFDC), are designed to help certain families whose total income falls below a federally determined minimum amount. The present amount is approximately $17,000 for a family of four. The larger the family, the more income is required and the more money is paid out. Critics have claimed that welfare provides an incentive for unwed mothers to have children or exploit the system.

The **Supplemental Nutritional Assistance Program** (SNAP, formerly known as **food stamps**) is administered at the state level to assist low-income families. Recipients use government-provided debit cards to help pay for food. Some recipients do not qualify for AFDC.

The **Welfare Reform Act,** passed in 1996, aimed to reduce the number of people living on public assistance. It did so by splitting funding for these programs across both the state and federal government, with the latter contributing the greatest share in the form of **block grants,** so as to allow the state to more readily experiment with programs that could end people's reliance on public assistance.

Fiscal Spending 〜

The government takes in a great deal of money each year. But those earnings must be balanced against all of the government's yearly expenditures. In the diagram below, review how the $3.9 trillion dollars the government had in 2016 was spent. On the next page, we'll take an even closer look at the discretionary spending segment.

2016 Spending

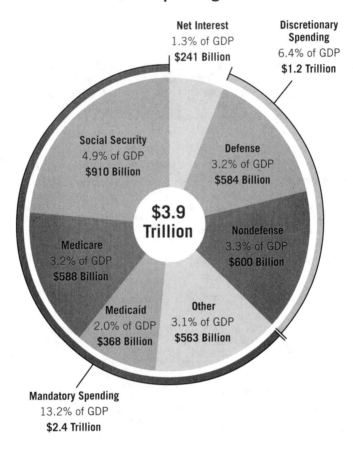

Net Interest
1.3% of GDP
$241 Billion

Discretionary Spending
6.4% of GDP
$1.2 Trillion

Social Security
4.9% of GDP
$910 Billion

Defense
3.2% of GDP
$584 Billion

$3.9 Trillion

Nondefense
3.3% of GDP
$600 Billion

Medicare
3.2% of GDP
$588 Billion

Medicaid
2.0% of GDP
$368 Billion

Other
3.1% of GDP
$563 Billion

Mandatory Spending
13.2% of GDP
$2.4 Trillion

Discretionary Spending for 2016

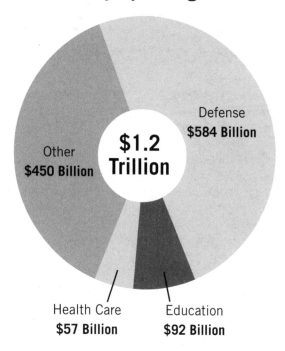

Defense
$584 Billion

Other
$450 Billion

$1.2
Trillion

Health Care
$57 Billion

Education
$92 Billion

Defense

What the Money Accomplishes: The United States spends more than virtually all other developed countries combined on national defense. This high spending is meant to support America's allies and intimidate rival nations.

Where the Money Comes From: 28% of all tax revenues goes to defense spending.

Major Changes in Expenditures: With the end of the Cold War in the early 1990s, defense spending plummeted 25%. Since the terrorist attacks on September 11, 2001, spending on defense has risen to its highest level in American history.

Education

What the Money Accomplishes: The federal government supplies around 8.5% of education funding, targeted mostly in the form of special education grants, Pell Grants, and education grants for veterans and their families.

Where the Money Comes From: 91.5% of funding for public schools in the United States is provided by local or state tax revenues. Most states fund public education through property taxes.

Major Changes in Expenditures: In response to the Soviet Union launching Sputnik in 1957, the federal government began directly funding American public schools. Since then, the federal government has given states financial incentives to implement federal educational policy. Programs such as Head Start and No Child Left Behind have propelled the federal government even further into the realm of public education.

Health Care

What the Money Accomplishes: Discretionary spending on health care goes toward research grants administered by the National Institute of Health, the Center for Disease Control, the Food and Drug Administration, as well as healthcare for Native Americans and veterans. (Medicare and Medicaid are funded through mandatory spending.)

Where the Money Comes From: Money for health care comes from employee payroll taxes.

Major Changes in Expenditures: The most significant health-care legislation in American history was signed into law by President Obama on March 23, 2010. The Patient Protection and Affordable Care Act (ACA), popularly known as Obamacare, provides federal subsidies to certain low-income families not already covered by Medicare through mandatory and discretionary spending. Since the legislation is new and subject to possible future repeal, it is unclear what its long-term impact on federal budgeting may be.

Other

What the Money Accomplishes: Money in the "Other" category funds scientific research grants, environmental and energy programs, and administrative costs.

Where the Money Comes From: Money for this category comes from income taxes.

Major Changes in Expenditures: When the presidency changes hands, the new president often adjusts the funding levels of these initiatives.

Deficit Spending 💬

When the government spends more than it takes in, it is left with a **budget deficit.** This additional spending is similar to the use of a credit card, with politicians borrowing (often from other countries) to meet the needs of the budget. This accumulated deficit is known as the **national debt.**

Money for deficit spending comes from selling Treasury Bonds, which give bearers a small amount of interest. Americans (private citizens, local governments, corporations) own 67.5% of America's debt. The remainder is owned by foreign governments.

Besides only a handful of occasions in which the federal government ran a surplus due to higher rates of taxation, the federal government has practiced deficit spending throughout its history.

Health Policy 〰

A government's social policy includes various initiatives that pertain to the health and living conditions of its citizens. In the United States, spending is largely aimed at initiatives that promote the safety of food, address public health emergencies, and promote medical research.

U.S. Department of Health and Human Services (HHS)

- A cabinet-level organization that deals with federally funded services like Social Security and healthcare, and whose Secretary works to directly advise the president.

Public Health Service (PHS)

- Manages a variety of other agencies, aiming to address anything that affects the public. Includes the Commissioned Corps, which is led by the Surgeon General.

Food and Drug Administration (FDA)

- Ensures the health of the American people by inspecting the food supply for contaminants and spoilage.
- Regulates the sale of over-the-counter drugs and patent medicines.

Centers for Disease Control (CDC)

- Works to prevent infectious disease, environmental contamination, and foodborne pathogens.
- In times of crisis, the CDC often makes recommendations to both physicians and citizens as to the proper course of action.

National Institutes of Health (NIH)

- Conducts biomedical research and also controls and administers federal money for medical research.

Regulatory Policy ❗

Government entities that are not within the 15 cabinet departments are called regulatory agencies. Regulatory agencies are given an extraordinary degree of independence from Congress and the president and are not as constrained by political pressure.

Business

Federal Trade Commission (FTC)
- Prevents fraud in the marketplace by preventing price fixing and deceptive advertising
- *In 2003, the FTC implemented a "Do Not Call" registry, which allows Americans to avoid telemarketing calls on landline phones.*

Securities and Exchange Commission (SEC)
- Protects investors by regulating stock markets and policing corporations to prevent false and misleading claims of profits
- *Since the banking crisis of 2008, the SEC has taken disciplinary action against a number of banks for both accounting fraud and providing misleading information to investors.*

Federal Communications Commission (FCC)
- Assigns broadcast frequencies, for licensing radio and television stations, and for regulating the use of wireless communication devices
- *The FCC is resposible for regulating nudity and obscenity on the public airwaves. After Janet Jackson's brief "wardrobe malfunction" at the Super Bowl in 2004, the FCC fined the CBS television network over $500,000.*

Labor

Occupational Health and Safety Administration (OSHA)

- Ensures workers are employed in a safe work environment

- *OSHA has approximately 2,400 inspectors covering more than 8 million workplaces where 130 million workers are employed. OSHA conducts over 80,000 inspections of workplaces per year.*

Equal Employment Opportunities Commission (EEOC)

- Enforces antidiscrimination laws

- *The EEOC was created after the Civil Rights Act of 1964, but has grown to protect workers in other categories such as national origin, religion, sex, age, and disability.*

Energy

Nuclear Regulatory Commission (NRC)

- Controls how electric power companies design, build, and operate nuclear reactors

- *After the 2011 Fukushima Daiichi nuclear disaster in Japan, the NRC promised to improve emergency standards for nuclear reactors to cope with a loss of power and to withstand floods and earthquakes.*

Federal Energy Regulatory Commission (FERC)

- Prevents price fixing and price manipulation in public utilities.

- *FERC is self-funding. It operates thanks to fees paid by the industries it regulates.*

Environment

Environmental Protection Agency (EPA)

- Enforces environmental laws passed by Congress, like the Clean Air Act of 1970, which aimed to reduce pollution from cars and, after amendment in 1990, also called for the replacement of ozone-unfriendly air-conditioner refrigerants.

- *The Endangered Species Act is intended to protect endangered wildlife habitats from human encroachment. To implement this goal, environmental impact statements are required whenever construction projects are planned.*

Economic Policy

A thriving economy is critical for any politician's approval ratings. Because the economy is so important to voters, officials are always looking for ways to improve key economic factors, such as the unemployment and inflation rates. However, the extent to which the government should act to influence the economy has been a central conflict in the U.S. and on the international stage. The chart on the next page describes four of the main theories of economics.

Laissez-Faire	Keynesian	Supply Side	Mixed Economies
• Government should never involve itself in economic issues; the market will reach a natural and efficient equilibrium if it is left alone.	• Government can smooth out business cycles by influencing the amount of income individuals and businesses can spend on goods and services.	• Government should cut taxes and spending on domestic programs to stimulate greater production.	• Capitalist systems are best owned by a combination of private and public (government) interests.
• Pursuit of individual profit serves the broader interest of society.	• A strong central bank is necessary to manipulate interest rates and the issuance of currency.	• The greater the number of goods, the less likely inflation is to occur.	• The price of goods and services should be determined by the free-market interplay of supply and demand, but the government should intervene in the case of market failure.
			• Profits should be kept by the owners and not shared.
"*Laissez-faire*," which means "let it be" in French, appealed to rugged individualists in the 19th century. Free-market economic systems are characterized by periods of prosperity followed by periods of economic contraction (also known as **boom and bust** or **bull markets** and **bear markets**.)	This model largely displaced the laissez-faire model after the **Great Depression** of the 1930s.	This model was in direct opposition to Keynesianism.	Whether they claim to be "capitalist" or "communist," modern governments use a blend of free-market policy government intervention to manage their economies.

Basic Economic Factors ❗

The prices of goods, services, and investments—and how rapidly those prices change over time—can influence the overall health of a nation's economy.

Inflation occurs when the value of the dollar decreases, and the relative cost of goods increases. **Deflation** is the opposite: the value of the dollar increases, and the relative cost of goods decreases.

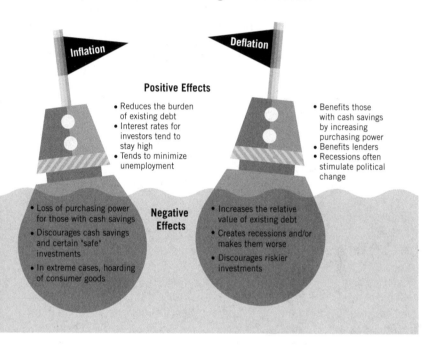

Inflation

Deflation

Positive Effects

- Reduces the burden of existing debt
- Interest rates for investors tend to stay high
- Tends to minimize unemployment

- Benefits those with cash savings by increasing purchasing power
- Benefits lenders
- Recessions often stimulate political change

Negative Effects

- Loss of purchasing power for those with cash savings
- Discourages cash savings and certain "safe" investments
- In extreme cases, hoarding of consumer goods

- Increases the relative value of existing debt
- Creates recessions and/or makes them worse
- Discourages riskier investments

Other Important Key Economic Terms

Hyperinflation—inflation that occurs so rapidly that consumers lose faith in the value of the nation's currency and often turn to gold or foreign currencies to seek stability.

Stagflation—a combination of high rates of inflation, slow economic growth, and high rates of unemployment. The United States experienced a period of stagflation in the late 1970s.

Fiat currency—a valueless currency declared to be legal tender (as opposed to money backed by gold or other precious metals). Fiat currency allows for manipulation of the economy by policy makers, but can tend to lead to inflation over time. All major currencies in the 21st century are fiat currencies.

 Ask Yourself...

Research the government's response after the beginning the Great Recession in 2008. What type of economic policy did the government use?

Monetary Policy

Monetary policy is a specific facet of economic policy and refers to the process by which the government controls the supply of money in circulation and the supply of credit through the actions of the **Federal Reserve Board** (the Fed), which works independently of the presidency. By controlling the supply of money and credit, the government hopes to be able to control inflation, deflation, and their effects.

The Fed can influence the amount of money in circulation by:
1. adjusting the discount rate (the lowest interest rate at which banks can give loans)
2. manipulating the reserve requirement (the amount of liquid cash banks must have on hand)
3. buying or selling bonds

Monetary policy can be implemented by the Federal Reserve Board in three binary ways:

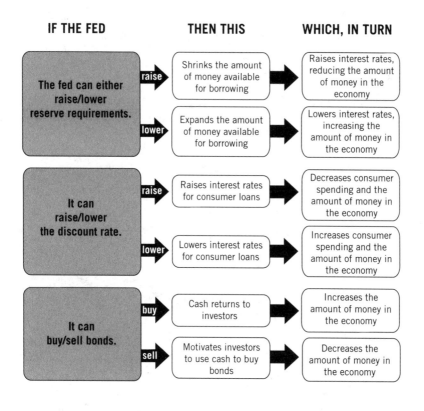

IF THE FED		THEN THIS	WHICH, IN TURN
The fed can either raise/lower reserve requirements.	raise	Shrinks the amount of money available for borrowing	Raises interest rates, reducing the amount of money in the economy
	lower	Expands the amount of money available for borrowing	Lowers interest rates, increasing the amount of money in the economy
It can raise/lower the discount rate.	raise	Raises interest rates for consumer loans	Decreases consumer spending and the amount of money in the economy
	lower	Lowers interest rates for consumer loans	Increases consumer spending and the amount of money in the economy
It can buy/sell bonds.	buy	Cash returns to investors	Increases the amount of money in the economy
	sell	Motivates investors to use cash to buy bonds	Decreases the amount of money in the economy

Some economists believe that government should intervene only to manipulate the money supply, an idea championed by **Milton Friedman**. These **monetarists** believe that the government should increase the money supply at a constant rate to accommodate economic growth. Monetarists do not believe that interest rate changes and the manipulation of tax rates have much of an impact on economic conditions.

Foreign Policy ❗

The foreign policy objectives of the United States have varied over the last 200-plus years, generally trending from isolationism to interventionism.

George Washington's Farewell Address (1797)

In his famous farewell address, Washington warned future presidents to steer clear of permanent alliances with any foreign nation. This philosophy is known as **neutrality.**

> "The Nation, which indulges towards another an habitual hatred, or an habitual fondness, is in some degree a slave."
> —George Washington

The Monroe Doctrine (1819)

The Monroe Doctrine was a policy of mutual **noninterference** with Europe. You stay out of the Americas, Monroe told Europe, and we'll stay out of your squabbles.

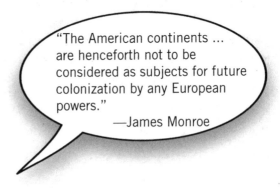

> "The American continents ... are henceforth not to be considered as subjects for future colonization by any European powers."
> —James Monroe

Imperialism (1890s to World War I)

The late 1800s were marked by the rapid growth of business **expansionism** into foreign markets. This encouraged a growing imperialism and acquisition of territories such as Hawaii, Puerto Rico, and Guam. The **Spanish-American War** and **Roosevelt Corollary** were applications of the new spirit of **interventionism**.

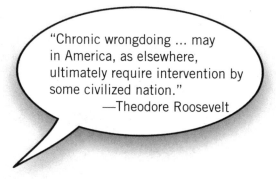

"Chronic wrongdoing ... may in America, as elsewhere, ultimately require intervention by some civilized nation."
—Theodore Roosevelt

Neutrality / Isolationism (1918–1942)

After the shock of World War I, the United States backed off on some of its previous imperialism and pursued subtler foreign policy measures such as the **Good Neighbor Policy** (regarding Latin America) and the **Neutrality Acts** (forbidding the sale of weapons to foreign countries).

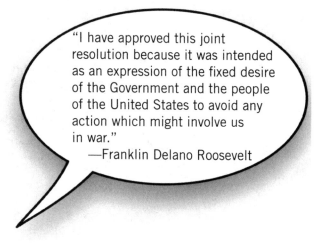

"I have approved this joint resolution because it was intended as an expression of the fixed desire of the Government and the people of the United States to avoid any action which might involve us in war."
—Franklin Delano Roosevelt

Cold War/Containment (post-World War II to 1980s)

After World War II, the foreign policy of the United States was dominated by the desire to contain the spread of Communism and limit the influence of the Soviet Union. The **Truman Doctrine, Korean War, Vietnam War**, and diplomatic efforts of President Ronald Reagan all reflect this vision.

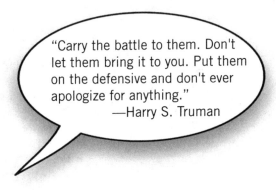

"Carry the battle to them. Don't let them bring it to you. Put them on the defensive and don't ever apologize for anything."
—Harry S. Truman

The War on Terror (2001 to present)

After the fall of the Soviet Union, United States foreign policy shifted from an emphasis on containment to an attempt to limit the influence of radical terrorist organizations in the Middle East. The "pre-emptive war" in Iraq, along with ongoing conflicts elsewhere, continues to represent a battle of wills rooted in religious, economic, and cultural differences.

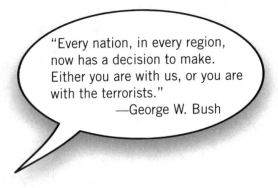

"Every nation, in every region, now has a decision to make. Either you are with us, or you are with the terrorists."
—George W. Bush

Diplomacy !

Foreign policy is set and implemented by four key players within and connected to the executive branch. When solving problems, **diplomacy** is always preferable to military conflict.

The **President** is the legal and ceremonial leader of America's foreign policy agendas. Presidents often meet with leaders of other nations in diplomatic efforts around the world. Ratifying a treaty requires the advice and consent of the Senate, but an **executive agreement,** which can be made directly with a foreign head of state, does not.

Any decision that the government makes affects large numbers of people, and the president, as the most public figure, takes the responsibility for anything that happens while in office. This causes presidential **approval** ratings to fluctuate drastically, and can have an impact on foreign policy agendas.

The **Secretary of State** is responsible for international relations. As the head of the **State Department,** the secretary coordinates a variety of activities concerning foreign relations. The State Department's **Foreign Service** includes **ambassadors** to more than 160 countries. Ambassadors manage **embassies,** which serve as a legal mouthpiece for Americans abroad. The **chief national security advisor** consults with the president on foreign policy matters. The responsibilities of the Secretary of State and the Chief National Security Advisor often overlap.

Increasingly, the State Department has pursued foreign policy agendas that seek to foster **globalization** and favorable **trade agreements.**

The **National Security Council (NSC)** is headed by the national security advisor, who has direct access to the president in matters relating to military and foreign policy. Since the late 1940s, the NSC has been involved in the decision-making process during national emergencies. Unlike the State Department, the NSC is largely free from congressional oversight. For this reason, it has become one of the most favored institutions of many presidents.

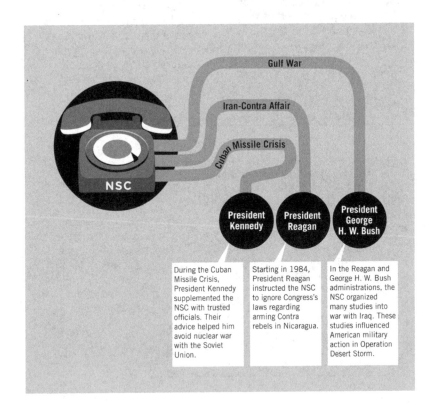

Gulf War

Iran-Contra Affair

Cuban Missile Crisis

NSC

President Kennedy

President Reagan

President George H. W. Bush

During the Cuban Missile Crisis, President Kennedy supplemented the NSC with trusted officials. Their advice helped him avoid nuclear war with the Soviet Union.

Starting in 1984, President Reagan instructed the NSC to ignore Congress's laws regarding arming Contra rebels in Nicaragua.

In the Reagan and George H. W. Bush administrations, the NSC organized many studies into war with Iraq. These studies influenced American military action in Operation Desert Storm.

The **Central Intelligence Agency (CIA)** gathers and analyzes information from foreign countries that might be of interest to the United States. Because many CIA operations are top secret, their activities may not go through normal channels and might not have an impact on approval ratings. The CIA director is appointed by the president and confirmed by the Senate.

Military Policy

In matters of military policy, the President, Secretary of Defense, and Joint Chiefs of Staff all play an important role.

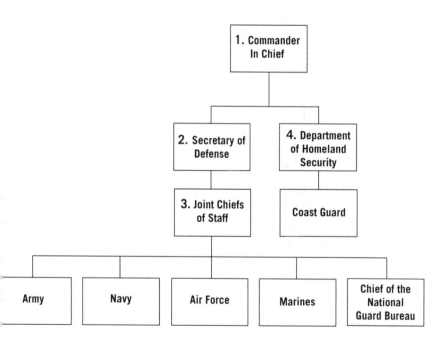

1. Commander in Chief

Article II, Section 2 of the U.S. Constitution states:

"The **President** shall be **Commander in Chief** of the Army and Navy of the United States, and of the militia of the several states, when called into the actual service of the United States; he may require the opinion, in writing, of the principal officer in each of the executive departments, upon any subject relating to the duties of their respective offices."

2. Secretary of Defense

The **Secretary of Defense,** who must be a civilian and who reports directly to the president, runs the **Department of Defense.** The President and Secretary of Defense work collaboratively to decide on military budget expenditures.

3. Joint Chiefs of Staff

The **Army, Navy, Air Force,** and **Marines** are each headed by a uniformed **chief of staff,** and the five chiefs work together as the **Joint Chiefs of Staff,** headed by a chairman. The Joint Chiefs and their chairman are responsible for carrying out defense policy and report directly to both the Secretary of Defense and the president. The military is therefore subject to civilian control.

4. Department of Homeland Security

Although the **Coast Guard** is one of the five branches of the military, the **Department of Homeland Security** controls it. Only in wartime does it operate under the auspices of the Navy.

The Role of the Bureaucracy and the Courts

Although regulatory agencies are, in theory, simply administrators, in practice they impact public policy through their alliances with other groups, like the iron triangles or **issue networks**, which are collections of interest groups and individuals. **Courts** likewise impact policy through rulings made on lawsuits.

The Process In Action

There is a large factory that is responsible for a lot of pollution. **Environmental regulations** have been proposed that would levy major fines against them.

A wealthy company might be able to afford paying the fines. One with marginal profits, however, would need to fight such regulations, as compliance might drive them into bankruptcy.

At stake are the livelihoods of all the other people who might depend on that company's survival. At the most immediate level, we're talking about the **jobs** of the employees, but there are also secondary industries that supply the company with raw materials and other labor. **Local government,** which relies on tax revenues from the company, also has an interest in the matter.

On the other side, speaking in favor of the regulations, are the concerned citizens and **environmental groups.** This complicated situation would certainly result in the creation of issue networks for the purpose of influencing the regulatory agency's decisions.

After all the opportunities for input and debate have been exhausted, the **regulatory agency** writes and publishes the rules (this is its **quasi-legislative** function).

If the industry still objects to the regulation, it can seek remedies in the courts by suing the regulatory agency. In the above example, if the company is forced to comply with the environmental laws, it could appeal the decision to the courts.

Important Linkages 💬

The formation and maintenance of public policy is almost never done by just one entity. Political parties, interest groups, public opinion, and other factors all help to form **policy networks** with common or conflicting goals.

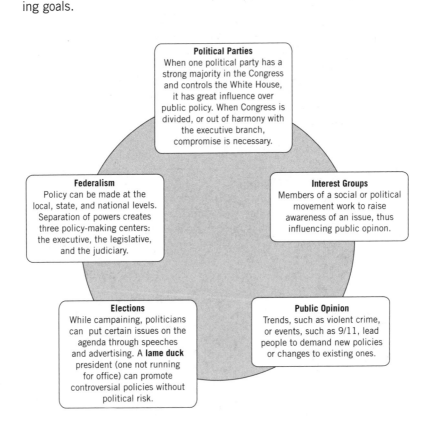

Political Parties
When one political party has a strong majority in the Congress and controls the White House, it has great influence over public policy. When Congress is divided, or out of harmony with the executive branch, compromise is necessary.

Federalism
Policy can be made at the local, state, and national levels. Separation of powers creates three policy-making centers: the executive, the legislative, and the judiciary.

Interest Groups
Members of a social or political movement work to raise awareness of an issue, thus influencing public opinon.

Elections
While campaining, politicians can put certain issues on the agenda through speeches and advertising. A **lame duck** president (one not running for office) can promote controversial policies without political risk.

Public Opinion
Trends, such as violent crime, or events, such as 9/11, lead people to demand new policies or changes to existing ones.

CHAPTER 6

Civil Rights and Civil Liberties

Civil rights and civil liberties exist to protect the people from an abusive government. This section reviews the civil rights granted by the U.S. Constitution, their interpretation by the Supreme Court, and how minority groups have fought for increased access to their civil rights over time.

The Bill of Rights

The Bill of Rights consists of the first ten amendments to the U.S. Constitution. These amendments provide the blueprint for civil rights in the United States, protecting people and states against abuses of federal power. The Supreme Court has, on many occasions, decided cases based on its interpretation of the Bill of Rights.

Rights vs. Liberties

Before jumping into the deep end with the Bill of Rights, review the difference between civil rights and civil liberties.

Civil Liberties

Specific freedoms the government cannot take away

(e.g., those numerated Bill of Rights)

Their Shared Goal

Protection from abuses of government power

Civil Rights

Equal treatment by the government, guaranteed by law

(e.g., no discrimination for race, gender, sexual orientation, and other protected classes)

The First Amendment ❗

The First Amendment is, at heart, about the freedom of speech, but that manifests itself in a variety of different forms.

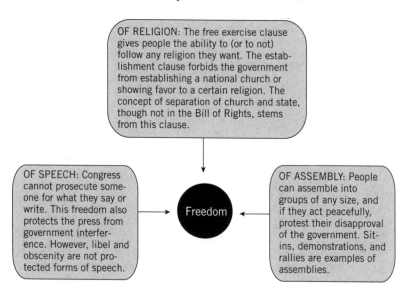

OF RELIGION: The free exercise clause gives people the ability to (or to not) follow any religion they want. The establishment clause forbids the government from establishing a national church or showing favor to a certain religion. The concept of separation of church and state, though not in the Bill of Rights, stems from this clause.

OF SPEECH: Congress cannot prosecute someone for what they say or write. This freedom also protects the press from government interference. However, libel and obscenity are not protected forms of speech.

Freedom

OF ASSEMBLY: People can assemble into groups of any size, and if they act peacefully, protest their disapproval of the government. Sit-ins, demonstrations, and rallies are examples of assemblies.

We Fight for the First Amendment 〰

To give an idea of how much America values its First Amendment rights, note the way in which President Roosevelt emphasized them in his January 6, 1941 "Four Freedoms" speech, given eleven months before America joined the Second World War:

> *In the future days, which we seek to make secure, we look forward to a world founded upon four essential human freedoms. The first is freedom of speech and expression—everywhere in the world. The second is freedom of every person to worship God in his own way—everywhere in the world.*

The Supreme Court Interprets the First Amendment

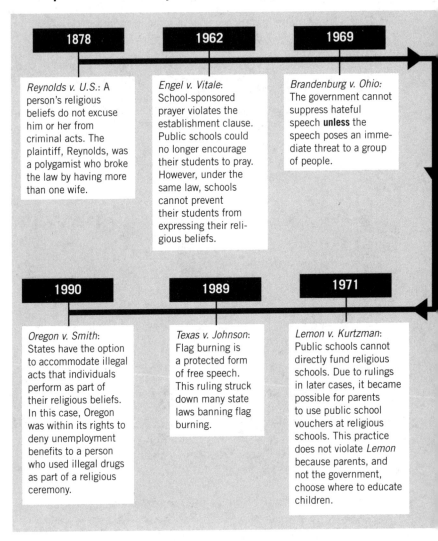

1878

Reynolds v. U.S.: A person's religious beliefs do not excuse him or her from criminal acts. The plaintiff, Reynolds, was a polygamist who broke the law by having more than one wife.

1962

Engel v. Vitale: School-sponsored prayer violates the establishment clause. Public schools could no longer encourage their students to pray. However, under the same law, schools cannot prevent their students from expressing their religious beliefs.

1969

Brandenburg v. Ohio: The government cannot suppress hateful speech **unless** the speech poses an immediate threat to a group of people.

1990

Oregon v. Smith: States have the option to accommodate illegal acts that individuals perform as part of their religious beliefs. In this case, Oregon was within its rights to deny unemployment benefits to a person who used illegal drugs as part of a religious ceremony.

1989

Texas v. Johnson: Flag burning is a protected form of free speech. This ruling struck down many state laws banning flag burning.

1971

Lemon v. Kurtzman: Public schools cannot directly fund religious schools. Due to rulings in later cases, it became possible for parents to use public school vouchers at religious schools. This practice does not violate *Lemon* because parents, and not the government, choose where to educate children.

Three times throughout American history, Congress has passed laws restricting people's freedom of speech, but in each case, the laws were either temporary (and expired) or were struck down by the Supreme Court.

- Sedition Acts (1798 and 1918): Restricted speech against the federal government during wartime.
- Smith Act (1940): Made it illegal to advocate the overthrow of the federal government. Used to prosecute American Communists.

Ask Yourself...

What are three ways that the Supreme Court has expanded (or retracted) people's rights through their rulings?

Impact of the Fourteenth Amendment 🛑

Besides the Bill of Rights, the Fourteenth Amendment (1868) has done the most to protect Americans' civil liberties and expand their civil rights. On many occasions since 1868, both the Supreme Court and Congress have used the Fourteenth Amendment to help many groups of Americans.

The Fourteenth Amendment ❗

Key Provisions

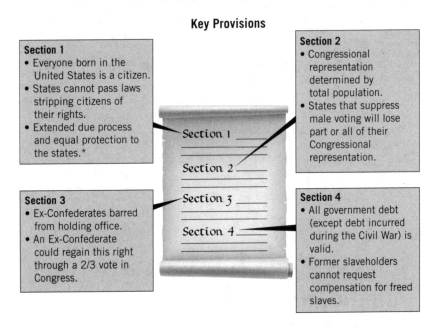

Section 1
- Everyone born in the United States is a citizen.
- States cannot pass laws stripping citizens of their rights.
- Extended due process and equal protection to the states.*

Section 2
- Congressional representation determined by total population.
- States that suppress male voting will lose part or all of their Congressional representation.

Section 3
- Ex-Confederates barred from holding office.
- An Ex-Confederate could regain this right through a 2/3 vote in Congress.

Section 4
- All government debt (except debt incurred during the Civil War) is valid.
- Former slaveholders cannot request compensation for freed slaves.

*The Fourteenth Amendment's Equal Protection Clause has had the greatest impact on Americans' civil rights. Through dozens of cases since 1868, the Supreme Court has used this clause to promote the selective incorporation of the Bill of Rights.

 Ask Yourself...

Why was Section 1 of the Fourteenth Amendment so influential in helping many groups of Americans expand their civil rights?

Selective Incorporation 💬

Two important rulings laid the groundwork for expanding American civil rights.

Case	Ruling and Effect
Barron v. Baltimore (1833)	The Bill of Rights restricts laws passed by the federal government, and not laws passed by states. States could pass laws infringing people's civil liberties.
Gitlow v. New York (1925)	States could no longer restrict people's right to free speech beyond what the Bill of Rights allowed. This is done under the constitutional doctrine of **selective incorporation**.

The Supreme Court was able to overturn *Barron* in 1925 due to the Fourteenth Amendment. One clause of the amendment holds that state laws must incorporate, or take into their own laws, civil rights guaranteed by the Constitution for all citizens. However, much debate has ensued regarding which rights in the Bill of Rights are included in the Fourteenth Amendment. In Gitlow, the Court selected First Amendment rights to be incorporated by the states.

In the discussion of civil rights movements to follow, pay close attention to which civil rights were selected and the circumstances under which they were incorporated.

Ask Yourself...

How does the Supreme Court's use of selective incorporation affect both civil liberties and civil rights?

African Americans Fight for Civil Rights ❗

From the end of the Civil War to the present, African Americans have fought for their civil rights. In the timeline, laws and Supreme Court rulings influenced by the Fourteenth Amendment are marked with an asterisk (*).

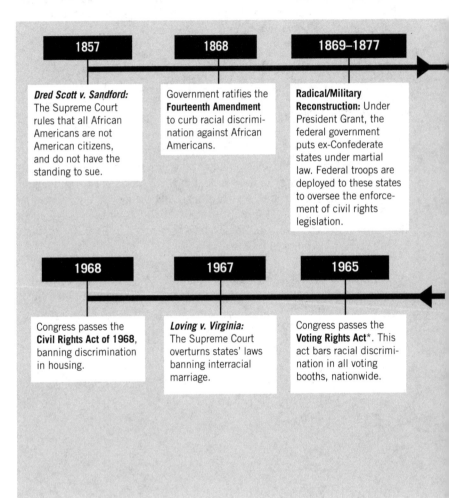

1857

Dred Scott v. Sandford: The Supreme Court rules that all African Americans are not American citizens, and do not have the standing to sue.

1868

Government ratifies the **Fourteenth Amendment** to curb racial discrimination against African Americans.

1869–1877

Radical/Military Reconstruction: Under President Grant, the federal government puts ex-Confederate states under martial law. Federal troops are deployed to these states to oversee the enforcement of civil rights legislation.

1968

Congress passes the **Civil Rights Act of 1968**, banning discrimination in housing.

1967

Loving v. Virginia: The Supreme Court overturns states' laws banning interracial marriage.

1965

Congress passes the **Voting Rights Act***. This act bars racial discrimination in all voting booths, nationwide.

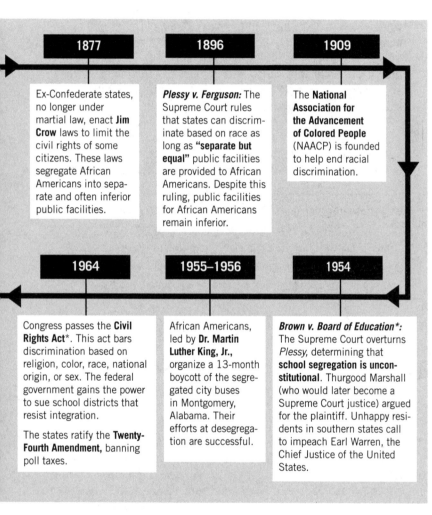

1877

Ex-Confederate states, no longer under martial law, enact **Jim Crow** laws to limit the civil rights of some citizens. These laws segregate African Americans into separate and often inferior public facilities.

1896

Plessy v. Ferguson: The Supreme Court rules that states can discriminate based on race as long as **"separate but equal"** public facilities are provided to African Americans. Despite this ruling, public facilities for African Americans remain inferior.

1909

The **National Association for the Advancement of Colored People** (NAACP) is founded to help end racial discrimination.

1964

Congress passes the **Civil Rights Act***. This act bars discrimination based on religion, color, race, national origin, or sex. The federal government gains the power to sue school districts that resist integration.

The states ratify the **Twenty-Fourth Amendment,** banning poll taxes.

1955–1956

African Americans, led by **Dr. Martin Luther King, Jr.,** organize a 13-month boycott of the segregated city buses in Montgomery, Alabama. Their efforts at desegregation are successful.

1954

***Brown v. Board of Education*:**
The Supreme Court overturns *Plessy,* determining that **school segregation is unconstitutional**. Thurgood Marshall (who would later become a Supreme Court justice) argued for the plaintiff. Unhappy residents in southern states call to impeach Earl Warren, the Chief Justice of the United States.

 Ask Yourself...

In the 20th century, what are three actions that African Americans took to expand their civil rights?

Lingering Effects of the Civil Rights Movement ❗

The Civil Rights Movement was much more than a collection of singular events. In some cases, positive change took decades and may still be continuing today.

- 1950s+: In the wake of *Brown*, some white families participated in what is now called **white flight**, moving to mainly suburban neighborhoods to avoid integration.
- 1960s+: In the early 1960s, the federal government started a program of **affirmative action**, giving black job applicants preferential consideration. College campuses across the country soon started a similar program.
- 1970s+: Since the 1970s, many school districts have implemented the practice of **bussing students** outside of their zoned schools to equalize each school's balance of students. This policy is extremely controversial, especially among Caucasian parents.

Though desegregation and bussing have had some success at integrating U.S. public schools, *de facto* (in fact) school segregation still exists throughout the United States, due to historically segregated school districts. *De facto* segregation is much harder to remedy because it is not *de jure* segregation, which is segregation created through law.

The Civil Rights Movement Expands ❗

Because the Constitution did not grant equal rights to all Americans, many groups have had to push Congress or the Supreme Court to belatedly do so. In the tables that follow, laws and Supreme Court rulings influenced by the Fourteenth Amendment are marked with an asterisk (*).

Power to the People!

Laws and Supreme Court rulings that advance social progress are not created in a vacuum. It is the political behavior of groups and individuals that spurs positive change. In the 19th and 20th centuries, many Americans stood up for the cause of advancing political and social equality.

Hispanic Americans

Issues/Discrimination Faced by Hispanic Americans	Supreme Court Rulings	Congressional Action
• High numbers of economic immigrants and refugees enter the United States from Central America, Cuba, and Puerto Rico over the course of the 20th century; many enter without legal documents or a clear path to citizenship. • Pushback against bilingual education in public schools. • Workers without citizenship are subject to low wages and unsafe work environments. Families are divided due to deportation.	Throughout the 20th century, the Supreme Court has ruled many times on the issue of bilingual education in public schools. As the court has changed its makeup, its position on bilingual education has shifted back and forth.	• Cuban Adjustment Act (1966): Eased immigration requirements for refugees fleeing Communist Cuba. • Jones-Shafroth Act (1917): Declares Puerto Rico a U.S. territory and its residents U.S. citizens.

PIVOTAL FIGURE: ◐

In the 1960s, Cesar Chavez, a farm worker and community organizer, co-founded the United Farm Workers (UFW), a labor union that appealed to Hispanic-American farm workers. In the mid-1960s, the UFW organized a five-year-long strike of grape pickers to protest low wages paid to Hispanic Americans. Like Mohandas Gandhi in India, Chavez participated in hunger strikes to show his solidarity with unionized farm workers.

> "We draw our strength from the very despair in which we have been forced to live. We will endure."
>
> —Caesar Chavez (1927–1993)

Successes: ◐

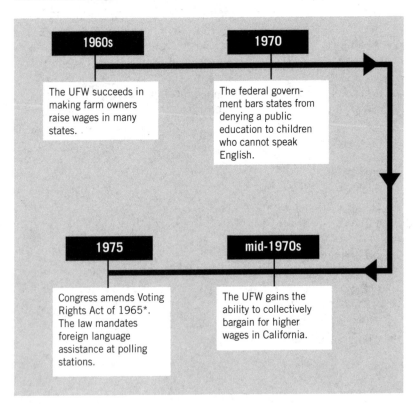

1960s	1970
The UFW succeeds in making farm owners raise wages in many states.	The federal government bars states from denying a public education to children who cannot speak English.

1975	mid-1970s
Congress amends Voting Rights Act of 1965*. The law mandates foreign language assistance at polling stations.	The UFW gains the ability to collectively bargain for higher wages in California.

Gay Americans

Issues/Discrimination Faced by Gay Americans	Supreme Court Rulings	Congressional Action
• Sexual relations between two people of the same gender was illegal in many states. • Marriage between two people of the same gender was prohibited through federal law, state law, and state constitutions.	• *Lawrence v. Texas* (2003)*: Struck down states' anti-sodomy laws. • *Obergefell v. Hodges* (2015)*: Upheld that states must issue marriage licenses to same sex couples under the Fourteenth Amendment, essentially providing gay couples with the fundamental right to marry.	• Defense of Marriage Act (1996): Defined marriage as a union between one man and one woman.

PIVOTAL FIGURE:

Nowhere in the United States was the push for gay rights and acceptance greater than in San Francisco. In the 1970s, Navy veteran and business owner Harvey Milk led a series of campaigns to provide gay Americans greater rights in the workplace. His tragic assassination in 1978 served to galvanize the gay rights movement throughout the United States.

" If a bullet should enter my brain, let that bullet destroy every closet door."

—Harvey Milk (1930–1978)

Successes: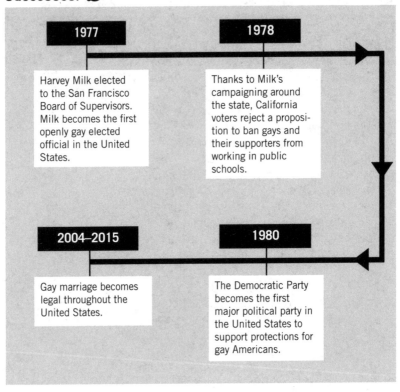

1977

Harvey Milk elected to the San Francisco Board of Supervisors. Milk becomes the first openly gay elected official in the United States.

1978

Thanks to Milk's campaigning around the state, California voters reject a proposition to ban gays and their supporters from working in public schools.

2004–2015

Gay marriage becomes legal throughout the United States.

1980

The Democratic Party becomes the first major political party in the United States to support protections for gay Americans.

Women

Issues/Discrimination Faced by Women	Supreme Court Rulings	Congressional Action
• Lacked the right to vote. • Fewer opportunities for employment and career advancement. • Lower pay compared to male workers. • Lacked access to birth control.	• *Griswold v. Connecticut* (1965)* : Defined the "right to privacy" in marital relations. • *Roe v. Wade (1973)* : Upheld that the right to privacy "is broad enough to encompass a woman's decision whether or not to terminate her pregnancy."	• Nineteenth Amendment (1920): Women gained the right to vote. • Title IX Education Act (1972): Barred sexual discrimination at schools receiving federal funding. • Lilly Ledbetter Fair Pay Act (2009): Expanded women's ability to sue their employers for unequal pay.

PIVOTAL FIGURE:

For much of late 19th and early 20th centuries, Susan B. Anthony was one of the most well-known figures of the women's suffrage movement. Arrested for attempting to vote in the 1872 presidential election, she spent her career lecturing throughout the country, converting more Americans to her cause. Although Anthony did not live to see the passage of the Nineteenth Amendment, she did witness many states extend voting rights to women before her death in 1906.

> "No man is good enough to govern any woman without her consent."
>
> —Susan B. Anthony (1820–1906)

Successes: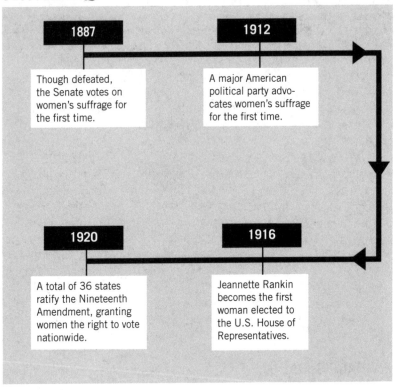

1887

Though defeated, the Senate votes on women's suffrage for the first time.

1912

A major American political party advocates women's suffrage for the first time.

1920

A total of 36 states ratify the Nineteenth Amendment, granting women the right to vote nationwide.

1916

Jeannette Rankin becomes the first woman elected to the U.S. House of Representatives.

Since the early 20th century, women have been fighting for the Equal Rights Amendment (ERA), a constitutional amendment that would bar all discrimination based on sex. Finally ratified by Congress in 1972, it failed because 4/5 of state legislatures did not ratify it. After the 2016 presidential election, however, there have been greater calls for Congress to pass the ERA, so states may try to ratify it once again.

Other Groups and Their Successes

Many other groups of Americans have fought for their civil rights. Below, review the discrimination these groups faced and the actions taken by the Supreme Court and Congress.

Group	Issues/Discrimination Faced by This Group	Supreme Court Rulings	Congressional Action
Native Americans	• Federal government signed and violated multiple treaties defining the boundary between Native American territory and the US. • Beginning in the early 19th century, the federal government used a combination of diplomacy, coercion, and violence to relocate Native Americans to reservations.	• *Worcester v. Georgia (1832):* The Supreme Court upholds the Cherokee Nation's right to exist within the state of Georgia. In an event known as the Trail of Tears, President Jackson has ignored the Court's decision and relocated the Cherokee westward.	• Dawes Act (1887): Gave financial assistance to Native Americans who left reservations and assimilated into American culture. • Indian Citizenship Act (1924): Granted U.S. citizenship to all Native Americans.

Group	Issues/Discrimination Faced by This Group	Supreme Court Rulings	Congressional Action
Asian Americans	• U.S. government interned approximately 120,000 Japanese Americans during the Second World War. • Approximately 130,000 Vietnamese, Laotian, and Cambodian refugees arrived in the United States at the end of the Vietnam War.	*Korematsu v. U.S.* (1944): The Supreme Court ruled that Japanese internment was legal, as it was not based on racial discrimination.	Indochina Migration and Refugee Assistance Act (1975): Allowed Vietnamese, Laotian, and Cambodian refugees to stay in the United States, and provided funding to help them adjust to their new lives.
Disabled Americans	• Difficulty accessing public facilities. • Difficulty finding employment.	**Not Applicable: No relevant court cases.**	Americans with Disabilities Act (1990)*: Businesses over a certain size must modify offices to make them accessible for disabled workers and clients.
Younger and Older Americans	• Older Americans not hired due to their age. • The military could draft young American men who lacked the right to vote.	**Not Applicable: No relevant court cases.**	• Age Discrimination Act (1967): Prohibits age discrimination in hiring. • 26th Amendment (1971): Lowered the voting age to 18.

Ask Yourself...

What was another group of Americans who faced discrimination and fought for political and social justice? What did they do, and what were their successes?

The Supreme Court's "Anticanon"

Like *Korematsu*, the Supreme Court has made other controversial decisions limiting the rights of Americans. In *Buck v. Bell* (1923), the Court ruled that Virginia could sterilize citizens it considered mentally unfit to reproduce. Today, *Buck* and *Korematsu* are part of the Court's "Anticanon," the worst decisions the Court has ever made. The Court has never overturned either decision.

Activist Organizations

Like with African Americans and the NAACP, the expanded civil rights movement resulted in many organizations that lobbied for greater civil rights. For example, in 1958, a retired teacher created the American Association of Retired Persons (AARP). AARP continues to lobby for the rights of older Americans.

Ask Yourself...

What are four legal roadblocks Americans have faced as they fought for civil rights?

A Closer Look at *Roe v. Wade* (1973)

"Roe" was the pseudonym of Norma McCorvey, a 21-year-old woman with two children. After learning that she was pregnant with her third child, she tried to obtain an abortion in Texas, where abortion was illegal except in cases of rape or incest. Unable to find an abortion provider, she enlisted the help of attorneys who took her case to the Supreme Court. The defendant in the case, Wade, was the district attorney of Dallas County, Texas.

In deciding the case, the Supreme Court considered two key questions.

Q: Did states' anti-abortion laws violate Americans' "right to privacy" that was established in *Griswold?*

A: Yes, states' anti-abortion laws violated the "right to privacy" pregnant women have with their doctors.

Q: If the Court legalized abortion, could states still restrict it?

A: Though the Court legalized abortion, the Court allowed states to restrict abortion beyond the first trimester.

In the decades since *Roe v. Wade*, this decision has split Americans across political lines. Protests for and against abortion are common in the United States, although it's important to note that they are far more complex than simply "for" or "against." On the one side, it comes down to being "Pro Choice"—having the right to determine what happens to one's body, especially when one's health is at risk. On the other side, which defines itself as "Pro Life," it comes down to the question of when life begins.

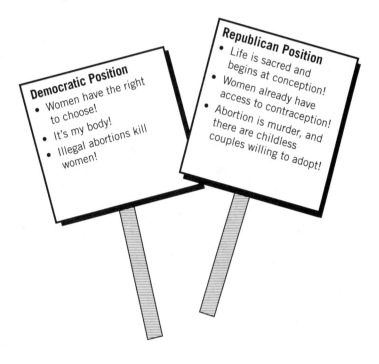

Democratic Position
- Women have the right to choose!
- It's my body!
- Illegal abortions kill women!

Republican Position
- Life is sacred and begins at conception!
- Women already have access to contraception!
- Abortion is murder, and there are childless couples willing to adopt!

President Johnson's Great Society 💬

The executive branch has also attempted to reduce discrimination and provide opportunity to historically oppressed groups of Americans. From 1964–68, President Johnson worked with Congress to legislate a series of programs known as the Great Society. These programs included the following provisions:

- Medicare and Medicaid to provide healthcare for older and disabled Americans
- Head Start educational programs for preschool-age children
- Food stamps
- Increased funding to public schools

Incorporating Rights of the Accused ❗

Miranda v. Arizona (1966) was only one of many Supreme Court cases that expanded the rights of criminal defendants. In the mid-20th century, Chief Justice of the Supreme Court Earl Warren led the charge to expand the rights of criminal defendants and all Americans. The decisions of the Warren Court continue to influence Americans' interactions with law enforcement and their government.

The Warren Court Reforms Justice ⚠

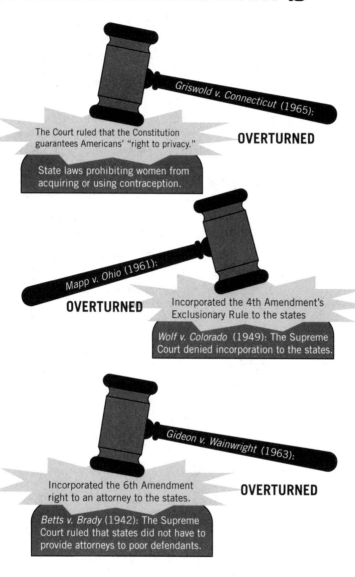

Griswold v. Connecticut (1965):

The Court ruled that the Constitution guarantees Americans' "right to privacy."

OVERTURNED

State laws prohibiting women from acquiring or using contraception.

Mapp v. Ohio (1961):

OVERTURNED

Incorporated the 4th Amendment's Exclusionary Rule to the states

Wolf v. Colorado (1949): The Supreme Court denied incorporation to the states.

Gideon v. Wainwright (1963):

Incorporated the 6th Amendment right to an attorney to the states.

OVERTURNED

Betts v. Brady (1942): The Supreme Court ruled that states did not have to provide attorneys to poor defendants.

Can the Government Suspend People's Rights? 💬

Although the Warren Court did much to expand people's rights, the Constitution gives the government the power to suspend certain rights. For example, the Constitution guarantees the people's right to *habeas corpus*: law enforcement must inform criminal suspects of the charges against them and bring suspects in front of a judge for legal proceedings.

Yet during a war or national emergency, the government can suspend *habeas corpus* so as to indefinitely detain thousands of people without pressing charges. The suspension of *habeas corpus* has happened only once on the national level, when President Lincoln imprisoned many Confederate sympathizers living in Maryland during the Civil War.

In World War II, the internment of Japanese Americans did not require the suspension of *habeas corpus*. Internment was achieved through President Roosevelt's Executive Order 9066. In 1942, Congress passed legislation supporting the executive order.

 Ask Yourself...

Why might some people believe that the government's ability to suspend the right to *habeas corpus* is a slippery slope?

The Constitution of the United States of America

Note: Text in *italics* indicates that a section of the Constitution is no longer in effect.

Preamble

We the people of the United States, in order to form a more perfect union, establish justice, insure domestic tranquillity, provide for the common defense, promote the general welfare, and secure the blessings of liberty to ourselves and our posterity, do ordain and establish this Constitution for the United States of America.

Article I

Section 1. All legislative powers herein granted shall be vested in a Congress of the United States, which shall consist of a Senate and House of Representatives.

Section 2. The House of Representatives shall be composed of members chosen every second year by the people of the several states, and the electors in each state shall have the qualifications requisite for electors of the most numerous branch of the state legislature.

No person shall be a Representative who shall not have attained to the age of twenty-five years, and been seven years a citizen of the United States, and who shall not, when elected, be an inhabitant of that state in which he shall be chosen.

Representatives *and direct taxes*[1] shall be apportioned among the several states which may be included within this union, according to their respective numbers, *which shall be determined by adding to the whole number of free persons, including those bound to service for a term of years, and excluding Indians not taxed, three-fifths of all other Persons.*[2] The actual Enumeration shall be made within three years after the first meeting of the Congress of the United States, and within every subsequent term of ten years,[3] in such manner as they shall by law direct. The number of Representatives shall not exceed one for every thirty thousand, but each state shall have at least one Representative; and until such enumeration shall be made, the state of New Hampshire shall be entitled to choose three, Massachusetts eight, Rhode Island and Providence Plantations one, Connecticut five, New York six, New Jersey four, Pennsylvania eight, Delaware one, Maryland six, Virginia ten, North Carolina five, South Carolina five, and Georgia three.

When vacancies happen in the Representation from any state, the executive authority[4] thereof shall issue writs of election to fill such vacancies. The House of Representatives shall choose their speaker and other officers; and shall have the sole power of impeachment.

Section 3. The Senate of the United States shall be composed of two Senators from each state, *chosen by the legislature thereof*,[5] for six years; and each Senator shall have one vote.

Immediately after they shall be assembled in consequence of the first election, they shall be divided as equally as may be into three classes. The seats of the Senators of the first class shall be vacated at the expiration of the second year, of the second class at the expiration of the fourth year, and the third class at the expiration of the sixth year,[6] *so that one third may be chosen every second year; and if vacancies happen by resignation, or otherwise, during the recess of the legislature of any state, the executive thereof may make temporary appointments until the next meeting of the legislature, which shall then fill such vacancies.*[7]

No person shall be a Senator who shall not have attained to the age of thirty years, and been nine years a citizen of the United States and who shall not, when elected, be an inhabitant of that state for which he shall be chosen. The vice president of the United States shall be President of the Senate, but shall have no vote, unless they be equally divided. The Senate shall choose their other officers, and also a President *pro tempore*,[8] in the absence of the vice president, or when he shall exercise the office of President of the United States. The Senate shall have the sole power to try all impeachments. When sitting for that purpose, they shall be on oath or affirmation. When the President of the United States is tried, the Chief Justice shall preside: And no person shall be convicted without the concurrence of two thirds of the members present.

Judgment in cases of impeachment shall not extend further than to removal from office, and disqualification to hold and enjoy any office of honor, trust or profit under the United States: but the party convicted shall nevertheless be liable and subject to indictment, trial, judgment and punishment, according to law.

Section 4. The times, places and manner of holding elections for Senators and Representatives, shall be prescribed in each state by the legislature thereof; but the Congress may at any time by law make or alter such regulations, except as to the places of choosing Senators.

The Congress shall assemble at least once in every year, *and such meeting shall be on the first Monday in December,*[9] unless they shall by law appoint a different day.

Section 5. Each House shall be the judge of the elections, returns and qualifications of its own members, and a majority of each shall constitute a quorum[10] to do business; but a smaller number may adjourn from day to day, and may be authorized to compel the attendance of absent members, in such manner, and under such penalties as each House may provide.

Each House may determine the rules of its proceedings, punish its members for disorderly behavior, and, with the concurrence of two thirds, expel a member.

Each House shall keep a journal of its proceedings, and from time to time publish the same, excepting such parts as may in their judgment require secrecy; and the yeas and nays of the members of either House on any question shall, at the desire of one fifth of those present, be entered on the journal.

Neither House, during the session of Congress, shall, without the consent of the other, adjourn for more than three days, nor to any other place than that in which the two Houses shall be sitting.

Section 6. The Senators and Representatives shall receive a compensation for their services, to be ascertained by law, and paid out of the treasury of the United States. They shall in all cases, except treason, felony and breach of the peace, be privileged from arrest during their attendance at the session of their respective Houses, and in going to and returning from the same; and for any speech or debate in either House, they shall not be questioned in any other place.

No Senator or Representative shall, during the time for which he was elected, be appointed to any civil office under the authority of the United States, which shall have been created, or the emoluments[11] whereof shall have been increased during such time: and no person holding any office under the United States, shall be a member of either House during his continuance in office.[12]

Section 7. All bills for raising revenue shall originate in the House of Representatives; but the Senate may propose or concur with amendments as on other Bills.

Every bill which shall have passed the House of Representatives and the Senate, shall, before it become a law, be presented to the President of the United States; if he approve he shall sign it, but if not he shall return it,[13] with his objections to that House in which it shall have originated, who shall enter the objections at large on their journal, and proceed to reconsider it. If after such reconsideration two thirds of that House shall agree to pass the bill, it shall be sent, together with the objections, to the other House, by which it shall likewise be reconsidered, and if approved by two thirds of that House, it shall become a law.[14] But in all such cases the votes of both Houses shall be determined by yeas and nays, and the names of the persons voting for and against the bill shall be entered on the journal of each House respectively. If any bill shall not be returned by the President within ten days (Sundays excepted) after it shall have been presented to him, the same shall be a law, in like manner as if he had signed it, unless the Congress by their adjournment prevent its return,[15] in which case it shall not be a law.

Every order, resolution, or vote to which the concurrence of the Senate and House of Representatives may be necessary (except on a question of adjournment) shall be presented to the President of the United States; and before the same shall take effect, shall be approved by him, or being disapproved by him, shall be repassed by two thirds of the Senate and House of Representatives, according to the rules and limitations prescribed in the case of a bill.

Section 8. The Congress shall have power to lay and collect taxes, duties, imposts and excises, to pay the debts and provide for the common defense and general welfare of the United States; but all duties, imposts and excises shall be uniform throughout the United States;

- To borrow money on the credit of the United States;
- To regulate commerce with foreign nations, and among the several states, and with the Indian tribes;
- To establish a uniform rule of naturalization, and uniform laws on the subject of bankruptcies throughout the United States;
- To coin money, regulate the value thereof, and of foreign coin, and fix the standard of weights and measures;

- To provide for the punishment of counterfeiting the securities and current coin of the United States;
- To establish post offices and post roads;
- To promote the progress of science and useful arts, by securing for limited times to authors and inventors the exclusive right to their respective writings and discoveries;
- To constitute tribunals inferior to the Supreme Court;
- To define and punish piracies and felonies committed on the high seas, and offenses against the law of nations;
- To declare war, grant letters of marque and reprisal,[16] and make rules concerning captures on land and water;
- To raise and support armies, but no appropriation of money to that use shall be for a longer term than two years;
- To provide and maintain a navy;
- To make rules for the government and regulation of the land and naval forces;
- To provide for calling forth the militia to execute the laws of the union, suppress insurrections and repel invasions;
- To provide for organizing, arming, and disciplining the militia, and for governing such part of them as may be employed in the service of the United States, reserving to the states respectively, the appointment of the officers, and the authority of training the militia according to the discipline prescribed by Congress;
- To exercise exclusive legislation in all cases whatsoever, over such District (not exceeding ten miles square) as may, by cession of particular states, and the acceptance of Congress, become the seat of the government of the United States,[17] and to exercise like authority over all places purchased by the consent of the legislature of the state in which the same shall be, for the erection of forts, magazines, arsenals, dockyards, and other needful buildings; and
- To make all laws which shall be necessary and proper for carrying into execution the foregoing powers, and all other powers vested by this Constitution in the government of the United States, or in any department or officer thereof.[18]

Section 9. *The migration or importation of such persons as any of the states now existing shall think proper to admit, shall not be prohibited by the Congress prior to the year one thousand eight hundred and eight, but a tax or duty may be imposed on such importation, not exceeding ten dollars for each person.*[19]

The privilege of the writ of habeas corpus[20] *shall not be suspended, unless when in cases of rebellion or invasion the public safety may require it.*

- No bill of attainder[21] or *ex post facto* law[22] shall be passed.
- *No capitation, or other direct, tax shall be laid, unless in proportion to the census or enumeration herein before directed to be taken.*[23]
- No tax or duty shall be laid on articles exported from any state.
- No preference shall be given by any regulation of commerce or revenue to the ports of one state over those of another: nor shall vessels bound to, or from, one state, be obliged to enter, clear or pay duties in another.
- No money shall be drawn from the treasury, but in consequence of appropriations made by law; and a regular statement and account of receipts and expenditures of all public money shall be published from time to time.
- No title of nobility shall be granted by the United States: and no person holding any office of profit or trust under them, shall, without the consent of the Congress, accept of any present, emolument, office, or title, of any kind whatever, from any king, prince, or foreign state.

Section 10. No state shall enter into any treaty, alliance, or confederation; grant letters of marque and reprisal; coin money; emit bills of credit; make anything but gold and silver coin a tender in payment of debts; pass any bill of attainder, *ex post facto* law, or law impairing the obligation of contracts, or grant any title of nobility.

No state shall, without the consent of the Congress, lay any imposts or duties on imports or exports, except what may be absolutely necessary for executing its inspection laws; and the net produce of all duties and imposts, laid by any state on imports or exports, shall be for the use of the treasury of the United States; and all such laws shall be subject to the revision and control of the Congress.

No state shall, without the consent of Congress, lay any duty of tonnage, keep troops, or ships of war in time of peace, enter into any agreement or compact with another state, or with a foreign power, or engage in war, unless actually invaded, or in such imminent danger as will not admit of delay.

Article II

Section 1. The executive power shall be vested in a President of the United States of America. He shall hold his office during the term of four years, and, together with the vice president, chosen for the same term, be elected, as follows:

Each state shall appoint, in such manner as the Legislature thereof may direct, a number of electors, equal to the whole number of Senators and Representatives to which the State may be entitled in the Congress: but no Senator or Representative, or person holding an office of trust or profit under the United States, shall be appointed an elector.

The electors shall meet in their respective states, and vote by ballot for two persons, of whom one at least shall not be an inhabitant of the same state with themselves. And they shall make a list of all the persons voted for, and of the number of votes for each; which list they shall sign and certify, and transmit sealed to the seat of the government of the United States, directed to the President of the Senate. The President of the Senate shall, in the presence of the Senate and House of Representatives, open all the certificates, and the votes shall then be counted. The person having the greatest number of votes shall be the President, if such number be a majority of the whole number of electors appointed; and if there be more than one who have such majority, and have an equal number of votes, then the House of Representatives shall immediately choose by ballot one of them for President; and if no person have a majority, then from the five highest on the list the said House shall in like manner choose the President. But in choosing the President, the votes shall be taken by States, the representation from each state having one vote; a quorum for this purpose shall consist of a member or members from two thirds of the states, and a majority of all the states shall be necessary to a choice. In every case, after the choice of the President, the person having the greatest number of votes of the electors shall be the vice president. But if there should remain two or more who have equal votes, the Senate shall choose from them by ballot the vice president.[24]

The Congress may determine the time of choosing the electors, and the day on which they shall give their votes; which day shall be the same throughout the United States.

No person except a natural born citizen, or a citizen of the United States at the time of the adoption of this Constitution,[25] shall be eligible to the office of President; neither shall any person be eligible to that office who shall not have attained to the age of thirty five years, and been fourteen years a resident within the United States.

In case of the removal of the President from office, or of his death, resignation, or inability to discharge the powers and duties of the said office, the same shall devolve on the vice president, and the Congress may by law provide for the case of removal, death, resignation or inability, both of the President and vice president, declaring what officer shall then act as President, and such officer shall act accordingly, until the disability be removed, or a President shall be elected.[26]

The President shall, at stated times, receive for his services, a compensation, which shall neither be increased nor diminished during the period for which he shall have been elected, and he shall not receive within that period any other emolument[27] from the United States, or any of them.

Before he enter on the execution of his office, he shall take the following oath or affirmation: "I do solemnly swear (or affirm) that I will faithfully execute the office of President of the United States, and will to the best of my ability, preserve, protect and defend the Constitution of the United States."

Section 2. The President shall be commander in chief of the Army and Navy of the United States, and of the militia of the several states, when called into the actual service of the United States; he may require the opinion, in writing, of the principal officer in each of the executive departments, upon any subject relating to the duties of their respective offices, and he shall have power to grant reprieves and pardons for offenses against the United States, except in cases of impeachment.

He shall have power, by and with the advice and consent of the Senate,[28] to make treaties, provided two thirds of the Senators present concur; and he shall nominate, and by and with the advice and consent of the Senate, shall appoint ambassadors, other public ministers and consuls, judges of the Supreme Court, and all other officers of the United States, whose appointments are not herein otherwise provided for, and which shall be established by law: but the Congress may by law vest the appointment of such inferior officers, as they think proper, in the President alone, in the courts of law, or in the heads of departments.

The President shall have power to fill up all vacancies that may happen during the recess of the Senate, by granting commissions which shall expire at the end of their next session.

Section 3. He shall from time to time give to the Congress information of the state of the union, and recommend to their consideration such measures as he shall judge necessary and expedient; he may, on extraordinary occasions, convene both Houses, or either of them, and in case of disagreement between them, with respect to the time of adjournment, he may adjourn them to such time as he shall think proper; he shall receive ambassadors and other public ministers; he shall take care that the laws be faithfully executed, and shall commission all the officers of the United States.

Section 4. The President, vice president and all civil officers of the United States, shall be removed from office on impeachment for, and conviction of, treason, bribery, or other high crimes and misdemeanors.

Article III

Section 1. The judicial power of the United States, shall be vested in one Supreme Court, and in such inferior courts as the Congress may from time to time ordain and establish. The judges, both of the supreme and inferior courts, shall hold their offices during good behavior, and shall, at stated times, receive for their services, a compensation, which shall not be diminished during their continuance in office.

Section 2. The judicial power shall extend to all cases, in law and equity, arising under this Constitution, the laws of the United States, and treaties made, or which shall be made, under their authority; to all cases affecting ambassadors, other public ministers and consuls; to all cases of admiralty and maritime jurisdiction; to controversies to which the United States shall be a party; to controversies between two or more states; between a state and citizens of another state;[29] between citizens of different states; between citizens of the same state claiming lands under grants of different states, and between a state, or the citizens thereof, and foreign states, citizens or subjects.

In all cases affecting ambassadors, other public ministers and consuls, and those in which a state shall be party, the Supreme Court shall have original jurisdiction. In all the other cases before mentioned, the Supreme Court shall have appellate jurisdiction, both as to law and fact, with such exceptions, and under such regulations as the Congress shall make.

The trial of all crimes, except in cases of impeachment, shall be by jury; and such trial shall be held in the state where the said crimes shall have been committed; but when not committed within any state, the trial shall be at such place or places as the Congress may by law have directed.

Section 3. Treason against the United States, shall consist only in levying war against them, or in adhering to their enemies, giving them aid and comfort. No person shall be convicted of treason unless on the testimony of two witnesses to the same overt act, or on confession in open court.

The Congress shall have power to declare the punishment of treason, but no attainder of treason shall work corruption of blood, or forfeiture except during the life of the person attainted.[30]

Article IV

Section 1. Full faith and credit shall be given in each state to the public acts, records, and judicial proceedings of every other state.[31] And the Congress may by general laws prescribe the manner in which such acts, records, and proceedings shall be proved, and the effect thereof.

Section 2. The citizens of each state shall be entitled to all privileges and immunities of citizens in the several states.

A person charged in any state with treason, felony, or other crime, who shall flee from justice, and be found in another state, shall on demand of the executive authority of the state from which he fled, be delivered up, to be removed to the state having jurisdiction of the crime.[32]

No person held to service or labor in one state, under the laws thereof, escaping into another, shall, in consequence of any law or regulation therein, be discharged from such service or labor, but shall be delivered up on claim of the party to whom such service or labor may be due.[33]

Section 3. New states may be admitted by the Congress into this union; but no new states shall be formed or erected within the jurisdiction of any other state; nor any state be formed by the junction of two or more states, or parts of states, without the consent of the legislatures of the states concerned as well as of the Congress.

The Congress shall have power to dispose of and make all needful rules and regulations respecting the territory or other property belonging to the United States; and nothing in this Constitution shall be so construed as to prejudice any claims of the United States, or of any particular state.

Section 4. The United States shall guarantee to every state in this union a Republican form of government, and shall protect each of them against invasion; and on application of the legislature, or of the executive (when the legislature cannot be convened) against domestic violence.

Article V

The Congress, whenever two thirds of both houses shall deem it necessary, shall propose amendments to this Constitution, or, on the application of the legislatures of two thirds of the several states, shall call a convention for proposing amendments, which, in either case, shall be valid to all intents and purposes, as part of this Constitution, when ratified by the legislatures of three fourths of the several states, or by conventions in three-fourths thereof, as the one or the other mode of ratification may be proposed by the Congress; provided that no amendment which may be made prior to the year one thousand eight hundred and eight shall in any manner affect the first and fourth clauses in the ninth section of the first article; and that no state, without its consent, shall be deprived of its equal suffrage in the Senate.

Article VI

All debts contracted and engagements entered into, before the adoption of this Constitution, shall be as valid against the United States under this Constitution, as under the Confederation.

This Constitution, and the laws of the United States which shall be made in pursuance thereof; and all treaties made, or which shall be made, under the authority of the United States, shall be the supreme law of the land;[34] and the judges in every state shall be bound thereby, anything in the Constitution or laws of any State to the contrary notwithstanding.

The Senators and Representatives before mentioned, and the members of the several state legislatures, and all executive and judicial officers, both of the United States and of the several states, shall be bound by oath or affirmation, to support this Constitution; but no religious test shall ever be required as a qualification to any office or public trust under the United States.

Article VII

The ratification of the conventions of nine states, shall be sufficient for the establishment of this Constitution between the states so ratifying the same.

Done in convention by the unanimous consent of the states present the seventeenth day of September in the year of our Lord one thousand seven hundred and eighty seven and of the independence of the United States of America the twelfth. In witness whereof We have hereunto subscribed our Names,

Signed:

G. Washington—President, and 38 representatives of the states

Notes

[1] This clause says that the government may only assess taxes on the states on the basis of population. Amendment XVI changed this by allowing the government to tax individuals' incomes.

[2] *Other persons* meant slaves. Amendment XIII abolished slavery, and Amendment XIV nullified the *three-fifths* clause.

[3] This is the clause that requires a national census every 10 years. The census is taken to apportion congressional representation; it is also used by Congress to decide how to distribute federal funding.

[4] The *executive authority* of a state is the governor.

[5] Amendment XVII changed this; senators are now elected by state voters, not by the state legislature.

[6] This section applied only to the first two Senates to guarantee senatorial elections every two years from the beginning of the Republic.

[7] Amendment XVII changed this by allowing the governor to make such temporary appointments.

[8] The president *pro tempore* presides over Senate when the vice president is not present.

[9] Amendment XX changed this date to January 3.

[10] *Quorum* means the minimum number of people required for the legislature to act. In other words, the Senate cannot begin a session unless at least 51 members are in attendance. Once a session has begun, however, the senators may leave the floor.

[11] *Emoluments* means payments.

[12] A congressperson cannot hold a second government job. This is a central component of the *separation of powers* within the U.S. government.

[13] The president's veto power.

[14] Congress can override a presidential veto with a two-thirds vote in both houses.

[15] This is called a *pocket veto* by the president. He does not return the bill to Congress, but because Congress has adjourned, the bill does not become law. Congress must then re-pass the law in its next session to force the president to consider it again.

[16] *Letters of marque and reprisal* allow private citizens to arm their boats so that they can attack enemy ships. In other words, Congress has the power to license private navies (called *privateers*). Given the circumstances of modern warfare, the chances that Congress will ever again exercise this power are small.

[17] This section refers to the District of Columbia (Washington, D.C.).

[18] This is the elastic clause.

[19] This section prohibited Congress from outlawing the importation of slaves until the year 1808. In 1808, Congress did in fact outlaw the import of slaves.

[20] A *writ of habeas corpus* is used by a defendant to appear before a judge, who determines whether the government has the right to hold the defendant as a prisoner. A defendant's right to a writ of habeas corpus is what prevents the government from arresting and imprisoning people without just cause.

[21] A *bill of attainder* is a law that finds an individual guilty of a capital offense (usually treason). Because it denies an individual's right to a fair trial, it is prohibited by the Constitution.

[22] An *ex post facto* law is one that declares an action a crime retroactively.

[23] Amendment XVI negated this section by altering Congress' power to impose taxes.

[24] Amendment XII overrides this section of the Constitution.

[25] This clause was inserted to provide for the first presidents, who as colonists had been born British subjects.

[26] This entire paragraph was modified by Amendments XX and XXV.

[27] *Emolument* means payment.

[28] This paragraph enumerates several key features of the system of *checks and balances.*

[29] Amendment XI prohibits an individual from using the federal courts to sue a state other than her state of residence.

[30] This paragraph says that if Congress finds a person guilty of treason, it may punish that person but not that person's descendants.

[31] States must accept the actions of one anothers' governments. Every state must accept every other state's driver's licenses, marriage licenses, legal decisions, and so on.

[32] The process described in this section is called *extradition.*

[33] This section refers to escaped slaves. It was nullified by Amendment XIII.

[34] This means that federal law takes priority when federal law and state law conflict. In *McCulloch v. Maryland*, Chief Justice Marshall interpreted this to mean that the federal government could nullify laws that contradicted federal law.

NOTES

The Princeton Review®

International Offices Listing

China (Beijing)
1501 Building A,
Disanji Creative Zone,
No.66 West Section of North 4th Ring Road Beijing
Tel: +86-10-62684481/2/3
Email: tprkor01@chol.com
Website: www.tprbeijing.com

China (Shanghai)
1010 Kaixuan Road
Building B, 5/F
Changning District, Shanghai, China 200052
Sara Beattie, Owner: Email: sbeattie@sarabeattie.com
Tel: +86-21-5108-2798
Fax: +86-21-6386-1039
Website: www.princetonreviewshanghai.com

Hong Kong
5th Floor, Yardley Commercial Building
1-6 Connaught Road West, Sheung Wan, Hong Kong
(MTR Exit C)
Sara Beattie, Owner: Email: sbeattie@sarabeattie.com
Tel: +852-2507-9380
Fax: +852-2827-4630
Website: www.princetonreviewhk.com

India (Mumbai)
Score Plus Academy
Office No.15, Fifth Floor
Manek Mahal 90
Veer Nariman Road
Next to Hotel Ambassador
Churchgate, Mumbai 400020
Maharashtra, India
Ritu Kalwani: Email: director@score-plus.com
Tel: + 91 22 22846801 / 39 / 41
Website: www.score-plus.com

India (New Delhi)
South Extension
K-16, Upper Ground Floor
South Extension Part-1,
New Delhi-110049
Aradhana Mahna: aradhana@manyagroup.com
Monisha Banerjee: monisha@manyagroup.com
Ruchi Tomar: ruchi.tomar@manyagroup.com
Rishi Josan: Rishi.josan@manyagroup.com
Vishal Goswamy: vishal.goswamy@manyagroup.com
Tel: +91-11-64501603/ 4, +91-11-65028379
Website: www.manyagroup.com

Lebanon
463 Bliss Street
AlFarra Building - 2nd floor
Ras Beirut
Beirut, Lebanon
Hassan Coudsi: Email: hassan.coudsi@review.com
Tel: +961-1-367-688
Website: www.princetonreviewlebanon.com

Korea
945-25 Young Shin Building
25 Daechi-Dong, Kangnam-gu
Seoul, Korea 135-280
Yong-Hoon Lee: Email: TPRKor01@chollian.net
In-Woo Kim: Email: iwkim@tpr.co.kr
Tel: + 82-2-554-7762
Fax: +82-2-453-9466
Website: www.tpr.co.kr

Kuwait
ScorePlus Learning Center
Salmiyah Block 3, Street 2 Building 14
Post Box: 559, Zip 1306, Safat, Kuwait
Email: infokuwait@score-plus.com
Tel: +965-25-75-48-02 / 8
Fax: +965-25-75-46-02
Website: www.scorepluseducation.com

Malaysia
Sara Beattie MDC Sdn Bhd
Suites 18E & 18F
18th Floor
Gurney Tower, Persiaran Gurney
Penang, Malaysia
Email: tprkl.my@sarabeattie.com
Sara Beattie, Owner: Email: sbeattie@sarabeattie.com
Tel: +604-2104 333
Fax: +604-2104 330
Website: www.princetonreviewKL.com

Mexico
TPR México
Guanajuato No. 242 Piso 1 Interior 1
Col. Roma Norte
México D.F., C.P.06700
registro@princetonreviewmexico.com
Tel: +52-55-5255-4495
+52-55-5255-4440
+52-55-5255-4442
Website: www.princetonreviewmexico.com

Qatar
Score Plus
Office No: 1A, Al Kuwari (Damas)
Building near Merweb Hotel, Al Saad
Post Box: 2408, Doha, Qatar
Email: infoqatar@score-plus.com
Tel: +974 44 36 8580, +974 526 5032
Fax: +974 44 13 1995
Website: www.scorepluseducation.com

Taiwan
The Princeton Review Taiwan
2F, 169 Zhong Xiao East Road, Section 4
Taipei, Taiwan 10690
Lisa Bartle (Owner): lbartle@princetonreview.com.tw
Tel: +886-2-2751-1293
Fax: +886-2-2776-3201
Website: www.PrincetonReview.com.tw

Thailand
The Princeton Review Thailand
Sathorn Nakorn Tower, 28th floor
100 North Sathorn Road
Bangkok, Thailand 10500
Thavida Bijayendrayodhin (Chairman)
Email: thavida@princetonreviewthailand.com
Mitsara Bijayendrayodhin (Managing Director)
Email: mitsara@princetonreviewthailand.com
Tel: +662-636-6770
Fax: +662-636-6776
Website: www.princetonreviewthailand.com

Turkey
Yeni Sülün Sokak No. 28
Levent, Istanbul, 34330, Turkey
Nuri Ozgur: nuri@tprturkey.com
Rona Ozgur: rona@tprturkey.com
Iren Ozgur: iren@tprturkey.com
Tel: +90-212-324-4747
Fax: +90-212-324-3347
Website: www.tprturkey.com

UAE
Emirates Score Plus
Office No: 506, Fifth Floor
Sultan Business Center
Near Lamcy Plaza, 21 Oud Metha Road
Post Box: 44098, Dubai
United Arab Emirates
Hukumat Kalwani: skoreplus@gmail.com
Ritu Kalwani: director@score-plus.com
Email: info@score-plus.com
Tel: +971-4-334-0004
Fax: +971-4-334-0222
Website: www.princetonreviewuae.com

Our International Partners

The Princeton Review also runs courses with a variety of partners in Africa, Asia, Europe, and South America.

Georgia
LEAF American-Georgian Education Center
www.leaf.ge

Mongolia
English Academy of Mongolia
www.nyescm.org

Nigeria
The Know Place
www.knowplace.com.ng

Panama
Academia Interamericana de Panama
http://aip.edu.pa/

Switzerland
Institut Le Rosey
http://www.rosey.ch/

All other inquiries, please email us at
internationalsupport@review.com